First World War
and Army of Occupation
War Diary
France, Belgium and Germany

21 DIVISION
110 Infantry Brigade
Leicestershire Regiment
6th Battalion
1 July 1916 - 31 March 1919

WO95/2164/1

The Naval & Military Press Ltd
www.nmarchive.com
Published in association with The National Archives

Published by

The Naval & Military Press Ltd

Unit 10 Ridgewood Industrial Park,

Uckfield, East Sussex,

TN22 5QE England

Tel: +44 (0) 1825 749494

www.naval-military-press.com

www.nmarchive.com

This diary has been reprinted in facsimile from the original. Any imperfections are inevitably reproduced and the quality may fall short of modern type and cartographic standards.

© **Crown Copyright**
Images reproduced by permission of The National Archives, London, England, 2015.

Contents

Document type	Place/Title	Date From	Date To
Heading	WO95/2164-1		
Heading	6th Bn Leicester Regt Jly 1916-Mar 1919		
Heading	6th Battn. The Leicestershire Regiment. July 1916		
War Diary	Humbercamp	01/07/1916	05/07/1916
War Diary	Talmas	06/07/1916	06/07/1916
War Diary	Hengest Sur Somme	07/07/1916	10/07/1916
War Diary	Fricourt	10/07/1916	16/07/1916
War Diary	Ribemont	17/07/1916	22/07/1916
War Diary	Leincourt	23/07/1916	26/07/1916
War Diary	Arras	27/07/1916	31/07/1916
Heading	Appendix I. (Narrative Of Action Of 6/Leicestershire Regiment 14th/17th July 1916)		
Miscellaneous	Appendix I Narrative Of Action Of 6th Leicestershire Regiment	25/07/1916	25/07/1916
Miscellaneous	War Diary		
Heading	1/6th Battalion Leicestershire Regiment August 1916		
War Diary	Arras	01/08/1916	31/08/1916
Heading	1/6th Battalion Leicestershire Regiment September 1916		
War Diary	Arras	01/09/1916	03/09/1916
War Diary	Liencourt	04/09/1916	18/09/1916
War Diary	Bernafay Wood	19/09/1916	30/09/1916
Operation(al) Order(s)	Operations On Somme From 25.9.16 To 30.9.16 Appendix II	08/10/1916	08/10/1916
War Diary	Bernafay Wood	01/10/1916	01/10/1916
War Diary	Somme	02/10/1916	17/10/1916
War Diary	Vermelles	22/10/1916	22/10/1916
War Diary	Trenches	23/10/1916	31/10/1916
War Diary	Vermelles	01/11/1916	02/12/1916
War Diary	Trenches	02/12/1916	03/12/1916
War Diary	Hohenzollern	04/12/1916	04/12/1916
War Diary	Sector	09/12/1916	15/12/1916
War Diary	Labourse	16/12/1916	19/12/1916
War Diary	Auchel	20/12/1916	28/01/1917
War Diary	Houtkerque	29/01/1917	31/01/1917
Miscellaneous	Entraining Table		
Operation(al) Order(s)	110 Inf. Bde. O.O. 43	27/01/1917	27/01/1917
War Diary	Houtkerque	01/02/1917	13/02/1917
War Diary	Chocques	14/02/1917	14/02/1917
War Diary	Bethune	15/02/1917	15/02/1917
War Diary	Novelles	16/02/1917	21/02/1917
War Diary	Vermelles	22/02/1917	05/03/1917
War Diary	Novelles	11/03/1917	11/03/1917
War Diary	Vermelles	17/03/1917	17/03/1917
War Diary	Lt Course	27/03/1917	28/03/1917
War Diary	Humbercamp	29/03/1917	30/04/1917
War Diary	Boisleux St Marc	01/05/1917	12/05/1917
War Diary	Berles Au Bois	13/05/1917	31/05/1917
Miscellaneous	Action at Fontaines-Les-Croisilles	03/05/1917	03/05/1917
War Diary	Berles-Au-Bois	01/06/1917	01/06/1917
War Diary	Moyenville	02/06/1917	07/06/1917

War Diary	Croisilles		08/06/1917	19/06/1917
War Diary	Moyenville		20/06/1917	20/06/1917
War Diary	Hendecourt Les Ransart		21/06/1917	30/06/1917
War Diary	Hendecourt		01/07/1917	01/07/1917
War Diary	Moyenville		02/07/1917	08/07/1917
War Diary	Croisilles		09/07/1917	03/08/1917
War Diary	Moyenville		03/08/1917	09/08/1917
War Diary	Croisilles		10/08/1917	17/08/1917
War Diary	Hamelincourt		18/08/1917	25/08/1917
War Diary	Gouy-En-Artois		26/08/1917	26/08/1917
War Diary	Manin		27/08/1917	16/09/1917
War Diary	Caestre		17/09/1917	23/09/1917
War Diary	Fontaine Houck		24/09/1917	26/09/1917
War Diary	Bedford House (Nr Dickebusch)		27/09/1917	27/09/1917
War Diary	Micmac Camp		28/09/1917	28/09/1917
War Diary	Nr Dickebusch		29/09/1917	30/09/1917
War Diary	In the Field		01/10/1917	30/11/1917
War Diary	Tincourt		01/12/1917	01/12/1917
War Diary	Villers-Faucon		02/12/1917	03/12/1917
War Diary	Epehy		04/12/1917	16/12/1917
War Diary	Villers-Faucon		17/12/1917	18/12/1917
War Diary	Saulcourt		19/12/1917	19/12/1917
War Diary	Epehy		20/12/1917	01/01/1918
War Diary	Saulcourt		02/01/1918	15/01/1918
War Diary	Lieramont		16/01/1918	20/01/1918
War Diary	Epehy		21/01/1918	31/01/1918
War Diary	Lepehy (Front Lines)		01/02/1918	01/02/1918
War Diary	Saulcourt		02/02/1918	04/02/1918
War Diary	Epehy		05/02/1918	07/02/1918
War Diary	Haut Allains		08/02/1918	14/02/1918
War Diary	Moislains		15/02/1918	18/02/1918
War Diary	Lieramont		19/02/1918	23/02/1918
War Diary	Saulcourt		24/02/1918	28/02/1918
Heading	6th Battn. The Leicestershire Regiment.March 1918			
War Diary	Epehy		01/03/1918	31/03/1918
Heading	1/6th Battalion Leicestershire Regiment April 1918			
War Diary	Allonville		01/04/1918	01/04/1918
War Diary	Locre		02/04/1918	02/04/1918
War Diary	Westoutre Area		03/04/1918	04/04/1918
War Diary	Kemmel		05/04/1918	08/04/1918
War Diary	De. Zon. Camp		09/04/1918	20/04/1918
Operation(al) Order(s)	Operation Order by Lt Col E.S. Chance Comdg Palm. Appendix VIII		22/04/1918	22/04/1918
War Diary			21/04/1918	30/04/1918
Operation(al) Order(s)	Operation Order No. 9 Appendix II			
Operation(al) Order(s)	Operation Orders No. 10 by Lt. Col. G.B. Chance Commdg. 6th Leic. Regt. Appendix III		06/04/1918	06/04/1918
Operation(al) Order(s)	Operation Orders No. 12 by Lt. Col. E.B. Chance Commdg. 6th Leic. Regt. Appendix IV		06/04/1918	06/04/1918
Operation(al) Order(s)	Operation Orders by Lieut Col E.S. Chance Comdg. Appendix IX			
Operation(al) Order(s)	Operation Orders No. 11 by Lt. Col. E.G. Chance Commdg. 6th Bn. Leic Regt. Appendix I		06/04/1918	06/04/1918
Operation(al) Order(s)	Operation Orders by Lt. Col. E.G. Chance Comdg. Palm Appendix V			

Operation(al) Order(s)	Operation Orders by Lieut Col E.S. Chance Comdg Palm. Appendix VII.	21/04/1918	21/04/1918
Operation(al) Order(s)	Operation Orders by Lieut Col E.S. Chance Comdg Palm. Appendix X		
Operation(al) Order(s)	Appendix VI	18/04/1918	18/04/1918
War Diary	Batt. H.Q. Swan.Chateau	01/05/1918	01/05/1918
War Diary	Bois. de Beauvoode	02/05/1918	02/05/1918
War Diary	Buysscheure	03/05/1918	04/05/1918
War Diary	Lagerty	06/05/1918	13/05/1918
War Diary	Hermonville	14/05/1918	14/05/1918
War Diary	In The Field Sector de Da Cote Between Cauroy Cormicy	15/05/1918	20/05/1918
War Diary	Chalons Le Vergeur	21/05/1918	31/05/1918
War Diary	Elnechy	01/06/1918	10/06/1918
War Diary	Moeurs	11/06/1918	11/06/1918
War Diary	Hangest	15/06/1918	16/06/1918
War Diary	Rambures	17/06/1918	21/06/1918
War Diary	Bazinval	22/06/1918	22/06/1918
War Diary	Le Mesnil Resume	30/06/1918	01/07/1918
War Diary	Arqueves	02/07/1918	17/07/1918
War Diary	Acheux P.15.d.2.8.	18/07/1918	31/07/1918
Heading	War Diary August 1918 6th Bn Leicestershire Regiment		
War Diary	Englebelmer	01/08/1918	05/08/1918
War Diary	West of Hamel	06/08/1918	17/08/1918
War Diary	Englebelmer	18/08/1918	20/08/1918
War Diary	NE. of Hamel	21/08/1918	22/08/1918
War Diary	Englebelmer	23/08/1918	31/08/1918
War Diary	Beaulencourt	01/09/1918	03/09/1918
War Diary	Villars-Au-Flos	04/09/1918	05/09/1918
War Diary	Sailly-Saillisel	06/09/1918	06/09/1918
War Diary	W of Manancourt	07/09/1918	07/09/1918
War Diary	Manancourt Equancourt Heudecourt	08/09/1918	08/09/1918
War Diary	Heudecourt	09/09/1918	15/09/1918
War Diary	Manancourt	16/09/1918	17/09/1918
War Diary	Heudecourt	18/09/1918	18/09/1918
War Diary	Peziere	19/09/1918	19/09/1918
War Diary	Etricourt	20/09/1918	24/09/1918
War Diary	Sorel-Le-Grand	25/09/1918	25/09/1918
War Diary	Gauche Wood	26/09/1918	29/09/1918
War Diary	Villers Guislain	30/09/1918	30/09/1918
Heading	War Diary 6th (Ser.) Batt. Leicestershire Regiment. From Oct. 1st To Oct. 31st 1918		
War Diary	Villers Guislain	01/10/1918	02/10/1918
War Diary	Gouzeaucourt	03/10/1918	05/10/1918
War Diary	Banteauzelle	06/10/1918	07/10/1918
War Diary	Montcouvez	08/10/1918	08/10/1918
War Diary	Meziere Fm.	09/10/1918	09/10/1918
War Diary	Caullery	10/10/1918	22/10/1918
War Diary	Amerval	23/10/1918	23/10/1918
War Diary	Vendigies-Au-Bois	24/10/1918	25/10/1918
War Diary	Poix Du Noid	26/10/1918	26/10/1918
War Diary	Orvillers	27/10/1918	29/10/1918
War Diary	Poix du Noid	30/10/1918	31/10/1918
Heading	War Diary Of 6th Bn Leicestershire Regiment. From 1st November 1918 To 30th November 1918		
War Diary	Poix de Noid	01/11/1918	02/11/1918

War Diary	Orvillers	03/11/1918	04/11/1918
War Diary	Futoy	05/11/1918	05/11/1918
War Diary	La Tete Noir	06/11/1918	06/11/1918
War Diary	Aulnoye	07/11/1918	07/11/1918
War Diary	Berlaimont	08/11/1918	11/11/1918
War Diary	Beaufort	12/11/1918	30/11/1918
Heading	War Diary Of 6th Bn Leicestershire Regiment. From 1st December 1918 To 31st December 1918		
War Diary	Beaufort	01/12/1918	13/12/1918
War Diary	Berlaimont	14/12/1918	14/12/1918
War Diary	Vendigies	15/12/1918	15/12/1918
War Diary	Inchy	16/12/1918	16/12/1918
War Diary	Guignemicourt	17/12/1918	31/12/1918
Heading	War Diary Of 6th Batt. Leicestershire Regiment. From 1st January 1919 To 31st January 1919		
War Diary	Guignemicourt	01/01/1919	31/01/1919
Heading	War Diary Of 6th Batt. Leicestershire Regiment. From 1st February 1919 To 28th February 1919		
War Diary	Guignemicourt	01/02/1919	06/03/1919
War Diary	Ferrieres	09/03/1919	31/03/1919

21ST DIVISION
110TH INFY BDE

6TH BN LEICESTER REGT
JLY 1916 - MAR 1919

from 37 DIV

110th Inf.Bde.
21st Div.

Battn. transferred
with Bde. from
37th Div. 7.7.16.

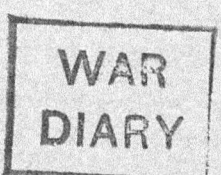

6th BATTN. THE LEICESTERSHIRE REGIMENT.

J U L Y

1 9 1 6

Attached:

Narrative of
Operations 14/17 July.

WAR DIARY or INTELLIGENCE SUMMARY

July 110/21 6 Queens
Vol V page
Vol 12

Army Form C. 2118

Place	Date	Hour	Summary of Events and Information	Remarks and references to Appendices
HUMBERCAMP	JULY 1st		The Battⁿ moved from SAULTY to HUMBERCAMP. The brigade being VIIth Corps Reserve.	
	2ⁿᵈ-5ᵗʰ		Remained in the huts at HUMBERCAMP.	
TALMAS	6ᵗʰ		The Battⁿ & 110ᵗʰ Bᵈᵉ transferred from 37ᵗʰ DIV to 21ˢᵗ DIV & moved by march route to TALMAS (17 miles). The 21ˢᵗ DIV belonging to 4 ARMY.	
HENGEST SUR SOMME	7ᵗʰ		The Battⁿ marched to HENGEST - SUR - SOMME.	
	8ᵗʰ			
	9ᵗʰ		The g.o.c. MAJ.GEN D.G.M CAMPBELL C.B. addressed the officers after B"	
	10ᵗʰ		The transport proceeded by road to MEAULTE The Battⁿ Reveillé 1=45 am & marched AILLY & entrained at 8 am, detrained at MERICOURT at 2.30 p.m. & taken in busses to MEAULTE, halted for 3 hrs. The Battⁿ proceeded to FRICOURT - the 1ˢᵗ line transport remained at MEAULTE	
FRICOURT	11ᵗʰ		The Battⁿ went into the trenches. A & B Coys in Support of QUADRANGLE TRENCH. B" HQᵣˢ & D Coys were in Reserve in FRICOURT WOOD.	
"	12ᵗʰ		Situation the same as above.	
"	13ᵗʰ		A & B Coys left the trenches at 3 p.m & bivouacked in SouthEastern edge of FRICOURT wood. Leaving here at 12 mid for the position of deployment at N.E corner of MAMETZ WOOD	
"	14ᵗʰ 15ᵗʰ 16ᵗʰ		The 110ᵗʰ Bᵈᵉ attacked & captured BAZENTIN-LE-PETIT Wood & village & welcome. APPENDIX I 5 sheets The action attacked 6ᵗʰ B" on right supported by 9ᵗʰ B". 7ᵗʰ B" on left supported by 8ᵗʰ B".	12 Z 5 sheets

WAR DIARY
or
INTELLIGENCE SUMMARY

Army Form C. 2118

Vol I

(Erase heading not required.)

Place	Date	Hour	Summary of Events and Information	Remarks and references to Appendices
RIBEMONT	17th		The battⁿ marched from FRICOURT WOOD at 7-45 p.m. to MERICOURT arriving at RIBEMONT at 12-30 A.M. 18th July	
	18th–19th		Reorganized battⁿ, cleared up & obtained equipment & obtained reinforcements to replace the fields of casualties handed into ordnance. The G.O.C. addressed the Bⁿ on recent action.	
	20th		The battⁿ entrained at RIBEMONT & detrained at SALEUX & marched to MONTEST	
	21st		The battⁿ proceeded to LONGPRE in lorries & bivouacked.	
	22nd		Marched thro' AMIENS to LONGEAU & entrained. detrained at ST POL & marched to MONCHEAUX & occupied billets	
LEINCOURT	23rd		Marched to LEINCOURT & occupied billets	
	24–26		LEINCOURT	
ARRAS	27th		Proceeded by motor lorry to IVANQUETIN & marched into ARRAS arriving about 10-30 p.m. & were billeted in the barracks.	
	28th		The 1st line transport went to MONTENESCOURT. The Bⁿ changed billets as follows. 1 coy of A coy occupied NICHOLLS REDOUBT ½ coy/A + C coy " cellars under BISHOPS PALACE B + D coys " the Nunnery in cellars Bⁿ H Q^s " MOAT & RAMPARTS	
	29–31		Same as above	

WAR DIARY
or
INTELLIGENCE SUMMARY

Army Form C. 2118

Vol II page 3

Place	Date	Hour	Summary of Events and Information	Remarks and references to Appendices
			At End of July Fighting Strength 26 Officers 370 O. Ranks. Total Strength 24 Officers 571 O. Ranks. 11 Officers joined on 29th July consisting total of 2 Officers on 23rd July making total of 24 Officers 1 Officer 24 July	

M. Wynward Major
1st Line Regt.

A P P E N D I X   I.

(Narrative of Action of
6/Leicestershire Regiment
14th/17th July 1916)

To:
  110th Inf. Bde.

APPENDIX I

Ref: C.G.A/G/597 d/24.7.16.

Narrative of Action of 6th
Leicestershire Regiment
From 3 a.m. 14.7.16 to 8 a.m. 17.7.16.

The Battn. moved from FRICOURT WOOD via the southern and eastern edge of MAMETZ WOOD and reached the N.E. Corner of this wood just before 3 a.m.

The Battn. was formed in four lines by 3.15 a.m. under a fairly heavy bombardment and lined up with the 7th Battn. on its LEFT about 100 yards in front of MAMETZ WOOD.

3.25 a.m. 1st and 2nd lines advanced on German first line, and five minutes later the third and fourth lines advanced, and, crossing first line, assaulted and took the German second line.

The first German line was very much knocked about and some 25 or 30 prisoners were taken in it. The Right Company blocked German first line trench on right of the attack, and also the same in the German second line.

While crossing "No man's" land the barrage was not very severe but the two right Coys. suffered a good many casualties from enemy machine-guns in BAZENTIN-LE-GRAND WOOD, which had not then been cleared by 7th Division on our right.

There were also two enemy machine guns in the S.E. corner of BAZENTIN-LE-PETIT WOOD. These were charged by the third and fourth lines and the detachments killed, and the guns taken.

There were not a large number of Germans in second line when it was entered.

The trenches had been so knocked about that it was difficult to consolidate them.

4 a.m. First and second lines, leaving small parties to deal with any dugouts, advanced to German second line, which was also being consolidated by the third and fourth lines.

4.20 a.m. Three platoons remained in German second line, and the rest of the Battn. advanced to the "One hour" line, which was reached after suffering a good many casualties from enfilade fire from the direction of BAZENTIN-LE-GRAND WOOD.

Soon after this the enemy, retiring in front of the 7th Divn. from BAZENTIN-LE-GRAND WOOD on our right, were enfiladed from the eastern edge of the wood by our Lewis Guns, and suffered heavy losses.

For some time the right Coy. had to form a defensive flank as many of the enemy were trying to get from BAZENTIN-LE-GRAND WOOD to BAZENTIN-LE-PETIT WOOD.

5.30 a.m. The Battn. advanced to the "Two hour" line and remained there till 6 a.m., waiting for the 7th Divn. to come up on the right. At 6 a.m. the Battn. was reinforced by several platoons of the 9th Battn.

At 6.5 a.m. the line advanced against the village, and, the LEFT of the 7th Divn. not being up, the whole village was assaulted and taken, and 3 Officers and some 200 prisoners.

P.T.O.

2.

At 6.40 a.m. the Royal Irish Rifles entered the village and the eastern portion was handed over to them.

7.15 a.m. The Battn. occupied and began consolidating the line from Northern end of village, thence Southwards to N.E. point of BAZENTIN-LE-PETIT WOOD, thence along Northern edge of wood halfway to the railway.

An attempt to get the real objective was heavily enfiladed from a point just outside the wood near the railway.

About 50 prisoners were taken in a trench along Northern edge of wood.

8.30 a.m. The enemy made a counter attack against the Northern portion of village. The 7th Divn. who were not very strong here fell back on cemetery.

The Battn. conformed and held Northern edge of wood and the prolongation of same through the village.

9.15 a.m. The 7th Divn. were reinforced and retook eastern portion of village, and the Battn. resumed its previous line, joining up with 7th Divn. N. of village.

3 p.m. The enemy made another counter attack against Northern and N.E. edge of village. Many of them reached the road running from N. end of village to railway and were at once stopped by our rifle and Lewis Gun fire.

The Battn. held and consolidated this position on the night of 14th and also on 15th there was no change.

At 2 a.m. on 16th a party of one Officer and 50 men were sent out to try and consolidate the original objective along the road. They were preceded by a party of One Officer and 40 men of the Yorkshire Regt. The latter party got to the road and held it for some time while our party was trying to consolidate, but were heavily bombed and enfiladed from enemy post just outside wood near railway, and was forced to retire.

On the night of the 16th the Battn. was relieved by the 10th K.O.Y.L.I. and the Battn. went into bivouac just south of FRICOURT WOOD, arriving there at 1 a.m. the 17th inst.

The Battn. suffered the following casualties.

   7 Officers killed and 20 wounded.
  500 O.R. Killed, Wounded, and Missing.

25.7.16.   Lieut. Col.
               Commg. 6th Leicestershire Regt.

WAR DIARY.

110th Brigade.

21st Division.

1/6th BATTALION

LEICESTERSHIRE REGIMENT

AUGUST 1916.

WAR DIARY
or
INTELLIGENCE SUMMARY
(Erase heading not required.)

Place	Date	Hour	Summary of Events and Information	Remarks and references to Appendices
ARRAS	AUG 1st 6th		A total of 225 men employed on working parties, chiefly on mine dugouts. A few shells fell into the town daily. Officers & N.C.O's attend courses - Gas, Grenade & Lewis gun under club arrangements.	
	7th		The Batt? relieved the 8th Batt? in the trenches & took over 98-101 trenches inclusive. The 7th B? relieved the 9th B? on our right. A Coy held 98-99, B Coy 100-101, C Coy in support, D Coy in redoubt line. NICHOLS - BOSKY redoubts & 2 platoons in Reserve.	
	8th 6 16-		Three days in the trenches were very quiet & much work was done on patrolling, no Germans were in front of the various defence lines. During this period there were no casualties.	
	17th		The Batt? was relieved by the 6th B? & A & B Coys went into billets in ARRAS. C Coy took over the defence of BOSKY, NICHOLS & FORESTIER redoubts D Coy — in B?e Reserve behind the CANDLE FACTORY. A rearrangement of the Brigade saw Tooth place 7th, 8th & 9th B? as holding the line & the 6th B? in ARRAS distributed as above.	
	18th 6 27-		Nothing of importance took place, a few shells fell daily into the town. Working parties of about 220 men were found daily. C Coy in the redoubt line only working in the neighbourhood of redoubts.	

WAR DIARY
or
INTELLIGENCE SUMMARY

Army Form C. 2118

Volume II   Page 5

Place	Date	Hour	Summary of Events and Information	Remarks and references to Appendices
ARRAS	27th		A draft of 9 men arrived.	
	28th		A Brigade school of instruction opened for grenadiers. Lewis gunnery. The Batt:- relieved the 7th/10th in the trenches. C Coy occupied support & reserve and B Coy right fire trenches. D Coy in support & A Coy in reserve. On 30th of Batt:- trenches received by 8th Leic: Rgt. On night of 31st Leic Rgt.	
	29th		Very quiet days in the trenches, the enemy only sending over a few small shells	
	30th		and a few rifle grenades.	
	31st		On 30th No. 25622 Pte H. Yeomby B Coy was killed. On 31st No. 25622 Pte H. Yeomby B Coy was killed.	
			Total casualties for the month 1 man killed.	
			The strength of the Batt:- 30 Officers 804 O.R.	

M. Willand Major
6 Leic R.F.

110th Brigade.

21st Division.

11

1/6th BATTALION

LEICESTERSHIRE REGIMENT

SEPTEMBER 1916.

Attached :- Report on Operations 25th to 30th.

WAR DIARY or INTELLIGENCE SUMMARY

Army Form C. 2118

(Erase heading not required.)

Place	Date 1916	Hour	Summary of Events and Information	Remarks and references to Appendices
ARRAS	Sept 1st 2nd 3rd		In sector ARRAS trenches, very quiet, only a few rifle grenades & shells daily	
	3rd		The batt'n was relieved by the 15th SHERWOOD FORESTERS (Bantams) & marched into billets at ARRAS & marched after dark to AGNEZ-les-DUISANS & billeted there.	
LIENCOURT	4th 5th		Marched to LIENCOURT & billeted	
	6th 12th		Batt'n cleaned up, bathed & all deficiencies made up. The batt'n trained, drill, route-marching etc	
	13th		Marched from LIENCOURT to PREVENT & entrained for DERNACOURT	
	14th		Arrived DERNACOURT & billeted. The 21st Div are in 4 ARMY.	
	15th		Marched to FRICOURT Camp via MEAULTE & BECORDEL	
	16th 17th		FRICOURT CAMP. The Bn marched to a bivouac on the N.W. corner of BERNAFAY WOOD. The W.Pd. 9/110th fd. moved here	
	18th		Arrived BERNAFAY WOOD & am strained hard	

Army Form C. 2118

Volume V page 7

WAR DIARY
or
INTELLIGENCE SUMMARY
(Erase heading not required.)

Place	Date	Hour	Summary of Events and Information	Remarks and references to Appendices
BERNAFAY WOOD	19th to 23rd		90 men engaged daily in building a Brigade H.Q. battle h.qt. The Battn employed on working parties, improving communications and support trenches.	
	23rd		On the night of 23rd the Battn dug assembly trenches between SWITCH TRENCH ready for the occupation of the Battalion on the 24th night	
	24th		All preparations & arrangements made for the attack against GUEDECOURT on 23rd	
	25th		The Battn moved up to assembly trenches at 4am 25th leaving 6 men behind to act as carriers	
			The operations from 25th - 29th appended.	appendix II
	29th		The Battn came out of the line on relief & bivouaced in same place as before the attack	
	30.		The total casualties in the attack were 3 officers killed 9 wounded 25 men killed 25 missing 149 wounded	
			The officers killed being Major Emmerson, Capt Gillett, & Lt Robinson. On working parties 7 killed & 31 wounded	

WAR DIARY
or
INTELLIGENCE SUMMARY

Army Form C. 2118

Volume V page 1

Strength Battalion 19 Officers 914 Other Ranks
fighting strength 19 Officers 540 Other Ranks

W. Whitehead Major
O/C 4th Can. Inf.

OPERATIONS ON SOMME FROM
25.9.16 to 30.9.16.

Appendix II

25th Sept. The Battn. started from BERNAFEY WOOD at 4 a.m., marched through DELVILLE WOOD, and occupied trenches as follows by 6 a.m.
    Headquarters and "D" Coy. - SWITCH TRENCH.
    "A", "B", and "C" Coys. - Assembly trenches behind SWITCH Trench.
The Battn. remained in these trenches till 1 p.m. (zero being 12.25 p.m.).
    At 1 p.m. "D" and "C" Coys. advanced across the open to follow up and occupy trenches vacated by 8th and 9th Battns. as they advanced, and to support and reinforce them in case of necessity.
    Two platoons of "D" Coy. and two platoons of "C" Coy. reinforced the 8th and 9th Battns. when they were checked by enemy machine guns in GIRD Trench, and they had a good many casualties from these machine guns, Major H.H. Emmerson (O.C. "C" Coy) being killed, and Captn. Quayle (O.C. "D" Coy) wounded.
    At 2 p.m. Headquarters and "A" and "B" Coys. advanced in artillery formation, as wounded men stated that the 8th and 9th Battns. were in the village.
    Battn. Headquarters were established in BULL ROAD Trench, and the Battn. was disposed as follows.-
    Two platoons of "C" Coy. and two platoons of "D" Coy. in PIONEER Trench, with oddments of 8th and 9th Battns.
    "A" Coy. and the remainder of "C" and "D" Coys. in BULL ROAD Trench.
    "B" Coy. in BULL ROAD support.
They remained in these positions during the night of 25/26th, and these trenches were very heavily shelled during the night.

26th Sept. The Battn. advanced at 4.30 p.m. preceded by patrols to take the final objective on the Northern and Eastern outskirts of GUEDECOURT. The barrage was fairly heavy and some few casualties took place.
    The leading platoons entered the village about 5.30 p.m. and the village was not then being shelled by the enemy.
    No enemy were encountered in southern portion of village, but the leading platoons, on reaching the LESBOEUFS-FACTORY CORNER Road through village, were heavily sniped and fired at by enemy machine guns. They held on to this line till dusk, when they were at once reinforced by the other platoons, and moved forward with very slight casualties to the orchards on the northern and eastern outskirts of village, and began consolidating. This was continued throughout the night with very slight molestation from enemy.
    The village itself and approaches to it, and especially its south-western edge were, however, very heavily shelled.
    Headquarters were established at N.26.d.2.8.
    Touch was established with 62nd Inf. Bde. on the RIGHT at N.27.a.5.0, but it was not till the morning of the 27th that connection was gained with the 55th Divn. on the LEFT.

27th Sept. Consolidation was continued as far as possible by daylight, and during the night the posts on the Northern edge were connected up. There was a certain

2.

amount of sniping, but the trenches were not heavily shelled. The village itself, and approaches to it were heavily shelled but very few casualties were sustained, as no troops were in the village.

28th Sept. Situation remained the same.
At midnight a strong patrol under 2/Lieut. J.B. Garner and a party of Pioneers went out to GARDEN Trench, and made a small post with blocks on either side to deny its occupation by the enemy.

29th Sept. Situation same.
At 7 p.m. the Battn. was relieved by 7th Inis. Regt. The relief was complete by 11.30 p.m.
A certain number of casualties were caused to both Battns. by enemy's bombardment of village and its approaches.

30th Sept. The Battn. returned to its former bivouac near BERNAFAY WOOD, arriving there at 1 a.m.

The casualties suffered by the Battn. during these operations, were as follows:-

OFFICERS.

Killed.
- Major H.H. Emmerson.
- Capt. G.M.G. Gillett.
- 2/Lt. W.E. Robinson.

Wounded:-
- Capt. G.A. Quayle.
- Lieut. A.V. Dagg.
- " F. Woolnough.
- 2/Lt. A.C. Nicholls.
- " C.H. Higson.
- " A.E. Dixon.
- " E.G. Lane-Roberts.
- " F.J. Hodgson.
- " F. Gilding.
- " G.H. Lowen.

OTHER RANKS.

Killed.	Missing.	Wounded.
32	25	141.

8.10.18.

Lt. Col.
Commg. 6th Leicester Regt.

6th Leicester Regiment
Vol III Volume V
page 1

15.2
2 sheets

WAR DIARY or INTELLIGENCE SUMMARY

Army Form C. 2118

(Erase heading not required.)

Place	Date	Hour	Summary of Events and Information	Remarks and references to Appendices
BERNAFAY WOOD SOMME	Oct 1st		In bivouac at BERNAFAY WOOD.	
	2nd		The 110th Bde marched to DERNACOURT & billetted	
	3rd		DERNACOURT.	
	4th		The Batt'n entrained at EDGE HILL STA. DERNACOURT & moved to LONGPRE near ABBEVILLE & then marched to COQUERILL & billetted	
	5th 6th		COQUERILL, all the men had baths & had a general clean up.	
	7th		Marched to PONT REMY & entrained for BETHUNE - marched to SAILLY LA BOURSE. The Brigade now in 1st Corps of 1st Army.	
	8th 9th		The Officers reconnoitred the trenches near VERMELLES.	
	10th		The batt'n relieved the 2nd R. Berks Regt in the trenches, the HOHENZOLLERN SECTOR, the order of the Brigade being 7th Leic. Regt on right & 6th Lept. front trenches, 9th B" in support, 8th in reserve. Much time taken up in trying to repair damaged trenches which were in very bad condition. Hostile minenwerfer fire severe and the Batt'n lost 3 killed & 12 wounded. R.V.	
	16th		The Batt'n were relieved by the 9th Batt'n & went into support line in RESERVE TRENCH	
	17th-21st		Very quiet, no casualties, & working parties found daily for Bn in front line On 18th the B's took over RAILWAY KEEP from 64th Bde on the left. Support Line being RAILWAY KEEP - CENTRAL KEEP - JUNCTION KEEP	

Army Form C. 2118

WAR DIARY
or
INTELLIGENCE SUMMARY
(Erase heading not required.)

Volume V
Page 2

Instructions regarding War Diaries and Intelligence Summaries are contained in F. S. Regs., Part II. and the Staff Manual respectively. Title Pages will be prepared in manuscript.

Place	Date	Hour	Summary of Events and Information	Remarks and references to Appendices
VERMELLES TRENCHES	Oct 22nd		The Bttn relieved the 9th K.R.R. in the front line.	
	23rd 24th 25th 26th		Very quiet. No casualties.	
	27th		Hostile minenwerfer very active causing much damage to trenches & many casualties in the Bttn. Our artillery retaliated with good effect.	
	28th		The Bttn was relieved by the 9th K.R.R. & moved into Reserve.	
	29th 30th 31st		The entire Bttn employed in working parties under the R.E. All men had baths & clean clothing. Form allowed passes to neighbouring villages.	
			During the month casualties have been 1 officer & 24 O.R. killed & 24 O.R. wounded. The strength of the Bttn being now 26 officers & 650 O.R.	

Wyfold Major
O.C. 9/Lincs R.

6th Division – Hqrs

Army Form C. 2118

Volume 5
page 3

Vol 16

16.2
2 sheets

WAR DIARY or INTELLIGENCE SUMMARY

Place	Date	Hour	Summary of Events and Information	Remarks and references to Appendices
VERMELLES	Nov 1st		In Reserve, Village line. Working parties of 350 men under R.E.	
	2nd		The batt⁰ relieved 9th batt⁰ in left sub sector front line trenches. B Coy on left, C on right, A in support, D in support. Relief complete at 11 am.	
	3rd		Quiet day.	
	4th		Capt Norty & 2/Lt Sittisbaner & Knighton. Sgt Mastin, Cpl Paynton were wounded.	
	5th		A & D Coys relieved B & C on front line	
	6th		Rain fell heavily, trenches fell in in many places.	
	7th		Still raining, very heavy falls – much labour needed. Trenches in very bad state.	
	8th		The batt⁰ was relieved by 9th B⁴ at 9.30 am. A & B Coys went into support holding line JUNCTION KEEP – CENTRAL KEEP – RAILWAY RES – RAILWAY KEEP.	
	9th		2/Lt KIRBY awarded M.C.	
	10th–12th		Working parties of 50 men supplied for front line batt⁰	
	13th		Capt & Adjt W.W. MAWSON returned	
	14th		The batt⁰ relieved 9th batt⁰ in front trenches sub sector left, relief complete 11 am	
	15th 16th		Quiet days, Gas alert.	
	17th		2/Lt BUCKLEY attached wireless R.E. struck off strength & est. plat⁰ having rejoined his own on oung to ill health.	

WAR DIARY
or
INTELLIGENCE SUMMARY

(Erase heading not required.)

Army Form C. 2118

Volume II page 4

Place	Date	Hour	Summary of Events and Information	Remarks and references to Appendices
VERMELLES	NOV 18		MAJOR W.H. YOUNG appointed 2nd in Comd. NOYELLES	
	19		Rained	
	20		Quiet day	
	21		Batt was relieved by 9th HB & marched into Reserve line. D Coy into billets in village	
	22		Gas alert cancelled	
	23		In Reserve. Working parties of 300 men supplied	
	26		Lt-Col C.E.G. Challenor awarded D.S.O.	
	27		The Batt relieved 9th Batt in Trenches	
	28		Lt-Col C.Y. Challenor took command of the Brigade during temp absence of Brigadier to England. Major R.H. Galland Bearing temp cmd of Batt	
			Quiet day in Trenches	
	29		The Batt is ordered to the South & rear-Batt from BOYAU 2 exclusive to LEFT coyau inclusive. The 10th Bde now on left of Batt	
	30		A + D Coys relieved B + C Coys in front line, enemy's artillery gave a line strength of Batt in Trenches 16 officers 392 O.R.	

R.H. Galland Major
Comdg 6 Leic R.E.

Army Form C. 2118.

6th Leicesh Regt. WAR DIARY or INTELLIGENCE SUMMARY.

Volume V page 5

Vol 17

17 2
3 sheet

Place	Date	Hour	Summary of Events and Information	Remarks and references to Appendices
VERNELLES TRENCHES HOHENZOLLERN SECTOR.	Dec 1st & 2nd		Very quiet both days.	
	3rd		The Batt'n was relieved by 9th Leic Regt & moved into support.	
	4 to 8		Very quiet days. No casualties. Working parties found for 8th & 9th B/ns in the trenches.	
	9th		The Batt'n relieved the 9th B'n in front line	
	9th 10th		Enemy's heavy trench mortars were active & QUARRY ALLEY blown in from a distance of 20 yds.	
	11th		Enemy's artillery more active than usual, which destroyed our kitchen & NCO's shelter in our support line. No casualties. The G.O.C. visited the trenches & the new tunnel system.	
	12th		Enemy artillery again very active, strong retaliation by our own guns. Early front officers of the 10th KOYLI reconnoitred the trenches. This being the battalion of the 6th Div.	
	13 & 14		The Batt'n was relieved by the 10th K.O.Y.L.I. relief complete at 3 p.m. The batt'n marched to billets at SAILLY-LA-BOURSE. 162 men to NOEUX LES MINES and 130 men to SAILLY. Four Coys (or Two) were attached to 17th Infan Bug R.E. & 253rd Tun Coy R.E. respectively. The batt'n had been 66 days continuously in the trenches of been there just [illegible]	

WAR DIARY or INTELLIGENCE SUMMARY

Army Form C. 2118.

Volume V Page 6

Place	Date	Hour	Summary of Events and Information	Remarks and references to Appendices
LABOURSE	16th		A much needed rest & clean up, baths for the men, new clothing issued.	
	17th			
	18th		Clean up continued. Intensive recovery. Hockey team. Received orders to move H.Q. & stores next day to AUCHEL	
	19th		All surplus kit moved to AUCHEL	
AUCHEL	20th		The Bn. reached AUCHEL distance 11 miles. The Bn. are billeted & the men carried on lorry. The working parties attached to R.E. are resumed rationed	
	21st &		Drill, P.T. Bayonet practice musketry	
	23rd			
	24th		R.E. parties rejoined batth.	
	25th		Xmas day. Church parade. The batth had dinner together in the local theatre. Letters were received from G.O.C. XIV.	
	26th		Men drilled etc & continued to clean up huts	
	27th			
	28th			
	30th		Lt. Col. C.R. Challoner resumed command after ½ years.	
	31st		The Bn. Band played OLD year out.	

6th Leic Rgt.

Volume V page 7

The strength of Batt'n on 31st Dec was 28 Officers 849 O.R.
The following officers wounded at BAZENTIN LE PETIT rejoined on 19.12.16
 Capt Y.C.A. COX
 2Lt SCHOLES
 2Lt BERNAYS

Maj YOUNG left Batt'n to join Medrane corps. 25/12/16
2Lt MUNN joined R.F.C. 20/12/16
2Lt PARR
2Lt KIRBY MCJ joined heavy machine gun corps.

DWGallwood Major
6th Leic Rgt.

6th Leicester Regt
Volume VI
May 1

WAR DIARY
INTELLIGENCE SUMMARY

Army Form C. 2118.

Place	Date	Hour	Summary of Events and Information	Remarks and references to Appendices
AUCHEL	1st		Batt'n training for 3 hrs Musketry, drill, P.T. bayonet fighting etc. Lewis gun classes shortly, Lewis gun, sniping, scouring	
	2nd		ditto & daily	
	3rd			
	4th		Lt Beamon came lectured 2 the brigade on his experiences as a prisoner of war in Germany	
	5th		The G.O.C. Division visited the training area	
	6th		The Corps Commander (1st Corps Gen Anderson) visited training area	
	7th		The batt'n paraded for church	
	8th		All recruits are fully trained in Musketry commenced a course on Inst. Musketry	
	9th		Col PALEY lectured to the battalion on the 2, 3rd Div. aerial formation	
	10th		The Army Commander (Horne) visited the training area	
	11th		Snow fell - weather very cold. Military sports in the Brigade commenced. The batt. (D Coy team) won Evelyn Wood competition. B Snipers won competition	
	12th		Lt Col BURNETT & GLADSTONE reported the battn	
			Heavy fall of snow	

Army Form C. 2118.

WAR DIARY
or
INTELLIGENCE SUMMARY.
(Erase heading not required.)

Volume VI Page II

Place	Date	Hour	Summary of Events and Information	Remarks and references to Appendices
AUCHEL	13th		Divine service, all Coys. fire on FOUFAY Range.	
	14th		Fell Church parade. National Church mission. After the service the Army Commander addressed the Brigade on the good work it has performed & Brigade. The latter then marched past.	
	15th		Signally competition. The Li: Corp 2" 3rd Sig Sec. 1st Batt: won cross country race.	
	16th		Transport competition our 2nd & 3rd Thirds	
	20th		Boxing competitions	
	21st		Church parade	
	22nd		Finals boxing. The boys won two 1sts. Lt. Col. E. H. CHALLENOR proceeded to England on leave. Maj. RAYNSFORD assumed command of the Batt. Route march start 8 miles.	
	23rd		Two Companies total 400 men proceeded to BARLIN to work on by-pass Railway under CANADIAN CORPS. The Lara foot-ball matches	
	24th		The Batt. won rapid wiring competition & 2nd in falling piece competition	

WAR DIARY
or
INTELLIGENCE SUMMARY.
(Erase heading not required.)

Army Form C. 2118.

Volume V

Place	Date	Hour	Summary of Events and Information	Remarks and references to Appendices
AUCHEL	JAN 25th		Companies carried on training as usual. C.O. visited Corps R.E. Pigeon Expert re advanced Batn. communications, arrangements.	
	26th		Signalling officer on one mile of front. Journal. Arrangements made for billeting balloon at Verguin.	
	27th		Early in morning orders for relief of French cancelled. Ordered to be here to move to HAZEBROUCK neighbourhood at short notice. Battalion ordered to march to billets and entrain.	
	28th		Arrived PROVEN station about 1 A.M. and marched in Coys to billets S.W. of HOUTKERQUE. Transport and working party at 4.50 from BARLIN arrived later.	
HOUTKERQUE	29th		Batn. Comdr. & O.C. Companies visited reserve system of trenches in preparation for moving up if required.	
	30th 31st		Normal. Physical training in morning & sports on ice in afternoon normal. Effective strength of Battalion 850 NCOs & men 33 officers.	

R. Fairlie C. Major
Comdg 6th Seaforth Regt.

ENTRAINING TABLE.

1st Personnel train

27th Leaves LILLERS. 17.47. arr. HAZEBROUCK
Jan.   18.34.

  Carries.   7 "B" Leic Reg.
             9 "B" Leic Reg.

2nd Personnel train

27th Leaves LILLERS 19.07. arr. HAZEBROUCK
Jan.   19.54.

  Carries.   6 "B" Leic Reg.
             8 "B" Leic Reg.
             Dismounted men. 98 F⁰ Coy. R.E.
             Dismounted men 63rd F⁰ Amb.

28th 1st Ominibus train. Leaves LILLERS 1.07.
Jan   arrives HAZEBROUCK 1.54

110 Bde. Hq.	6. Offr.	14. O.R.	9 horses	1 G.S. limb.
Signal Sect.	1 Offr.	26 O.R.	7 horses	1 G.S. limber
Lewis gun Det's Transport, 4 limbers G.S. wagons per B"		32 O.R.	32 horses	16 G.S. limbers
S.A.A. one limbered G.S. wagon per B"		4 O.R.	8 horses.	4 G.S. limbers
Two cookers per B"		8. O.R.	16 horses.	8 cookers.
One mess Cart per B"		4. O.R.	4 horses	4 carts
Eleven chargers per B"		44 O.R.	44 horses	
Nine pack animals per B"		36 O.R.	36 horses.	
Medical personnel with one maltese cart per Batt'n	4 officers (M.O?)	8. O.R.	4 horses	4 carts

1st Omnibus Train (con)
— The one Officer and 50 OR of "B" waving 2.
party will travel by this train.

Note to 1st Omnibus Train

Battalions which have not received the
fourth G.S. limbered wagon, but are in
possession of more than 12 Lewis
gun carts will take sufficient handcarts
(not exceeding six) for the use of the additional
guns.

25 Jan   Second Omnibus Train leaves
LILLERS 4.07 on HAZEBROUCK 4.54.

Two companies <u>6" B" Leic Regt</u>
<u>110 M.G. Coy</u> (less train transport) viz:-
10 Officers, 154 OR, 56 horses, 12 G.S.
limbered wagons, 2 carts.
<u>110. T.M. Bty.</u>

Two limbered tool carts per B" — 8 OR, 16 horses, 8 wagons
Two Cookers per B"   8 OR, 16 horses & cookers
Two water carts per B"   8 OR, 16 horses, 8 carts

16 hand carts and 8 motors of the 110
T.M. Bty. will be carried by this
train.

110 Inf. Bde. O.O. 43.   Copy No. 2.
Ref map   Jan 27" 1917
HAZEBROUCK 1/100000.

I. The 110. Inf. Bde. group will entrain in accordance with the attached Table.

II. Troops will move with one days Iron Ration, and the unexpired portion of the current days ration.

III. Blankets will be taken to LILLERS Railway Station in Lorries. One blanket per man to be taken on the train with men, all the second blankets to go on first Omnibus Train. Blankets to be rolled up in bundles of ten.
A loading party of 1. N.C.O. and ten men per Battalion will be left in charge of the 2nd Blanket per man.

IV. The 6" Batt" Leic Reg will detail a party of 1. Officer and 50 O.R. to load the first omnibus train.

V. ~~Infantry~~ Troops will arrive at LILLERS Station ½ an hour before train departure time. Transport will arrive

2.

T. (con).
three hours before train departure time.

AW Heinekker Major
B.M. 110 Inf Bde

Issued at 11:10am.

Copy No 1. to 6th B. Leic Reg.
     2.   7 B. Leic Reg
     3.   8 B. Leic Reg
     4.   9 B. Leic Reg
     5.   110 M.G. Coy.
     6.   110 T.M. Bty
     7.   98 F.d Coy RE
     8.   63 F.d Amb.
     9.   File.

6th Leicester Rgt
21st Division
Volume VI Page 4

Vol 19

19 2
3 sheet

WAR DIARY or INTELLIGENCE SUMMARY

Army Form C. 2118.

Place	Date	Hour	Summary of Events and Information	Remarks and references to Appendices
	February	1st	Normal	
HOUTKERQUE	2nd	2.30/4.00	8th Corps Commander, Gen: Hunter-Weston visited the Battalion	
		6.45/8.00	Bayonet training	
	3rd	2.30pm	Route march of Battalion and first line transport via	
		6	WATOU to JAN-TEN-BIEZEN. Reached en route by 2nd Army	
		6.45	Commander General Plumer, at WATOU	
	4th		Draft of 2 & 1 Officer & 66 men arrived	
			Route march repeated. Draft of 10 men arrived. Defences	
	5th		of YPRES reconnoitred by Commanding Officer	
	6th	10.30AM	Route march repeated.	
	7th	2.15PM	Cat turn out.	
	8th		Normal	
	9th	12.15PM	Brigadier presented Montenegrin Medal to Private F. Ceremony stretcher-bearer, for gallantry in the field	
	10th		Normal	

Army Form C. 2118.

WAR DIARY
or
INTELLIGENCE SUMMARY.
(Erase heading not required)

Volume VI Page 5

Place	Date	Hour	Summary of Events and Information	Remarks and references to Appendices
HAVERNE	February 11th		Billeting party proceeded to CHOCQUES	
	12th		Normal	
	13th		Battalion proceeded to CHOCQUES by 8.20 AM train from PROVEN	
CHOCQUES	14th		Battalion proceeded to BETHUNE, Montmorency Barracks	
BETHUNE	15th		Battalion proceeded to NOEULLES. A Coy. of Surplus LANCASHIRE	
			TRENCH	
NOEULLES	16th		Normal. Working party sent to VERMELLES Trenches each night	
	17th		Normal. One wounded.	
	18th		Normal.	
	19th		Batn. Commdr. & Company officers reconnoitred Trenches	
			in preparation for relief of 9th Battalion Yorks & Lancs Regt.	
	20th		Platoon officers reconnoitred trenches.	
	21st		Battalion relieved 9th Yorks & Lancs on left of Bry. sector. Relief	
			very difficult owing to state of trenches. 2 wounded during relief.	
VERMELLES	22nd		Normal. Trench warfare. One wounded on 22nd & 1 wounded	
	23rd			

WAR DIARY or INTELLIGENCE SUMMARY

Army Form C. 2118.

Volume VI Page 6

Place	Date	Hour	Summary of Events and Information	Remarks and references to Appendices
	February			
	26th	12MN to 1.30AM	At midnight of 25th heavy T.M. bombardment by enemy. Our artillery effectively replied. 3 killed 6 wounded and 1 died of wounds.	
	27th		Battalion moved into auditor.	
	28th		Headquarters moved to 62 headquarters of 194th battalion in conformity with extension of Brigade frontage to right.	
			Strength 47 OR arrived 25. 2.17	
			50 20. 2.17	
			7 19. 2.17	
			27 28. 2.17	
			2nd Lieut J— 7 officers arrived during the month.	
			Effective Strength 1018 OR 39 Officers.	
			A.R. Edwards 2nd Lt. Adjutant	

6th K Rif Rgt. March 1917

Army Form C. 2118.

WAR DIARY
INTELLIGENCE SUMMARY

Place	Date	Hour	Summary of Events and Information	Remarks and references to Appendices
VERMELLES	1st		Battalion in support trenches. Normal	
	2nd 3rd 4th 5th		Normal	
			Battalion moved into front line. Hohenzollern sector and relieved 9th Battalion	
			10 Battalion moved into reserve at Noyelles 2 Coys to Cambrin training and trenches	
NOYELLES	11th			
VERMELLES	14th		Returned to front line. Hohenzollern sector	
BURBE	27th		The Battalion left the front line for	
LA BOURSE			first line transport left for Humbercamp	
	28th		evening of 29th	
HUMBERCAMP	29th 30th 31st		Battalion moved to Humbercamp & Westhumbercamp intended for next line Battalion training out of trenches	

21/110

6th Bn Leicester Regt

Oct 21

WAR DIARY
or
INTELLIGENCE SUMMARY.

Army Form C. 2118.

Place	Date	Hour	Summary of Events and Information	Remarks and references to Appendices
Hem'court camp	Oct 1,2		6th in camp at Hem'court. Training under the Co. per Organisation.	
"	Apr 3		Bn moved at 9.15 am to Hamelincourt. Arrived at Hamelincourt & was put temporarily under the orders of the 62nd Bde.	
"	Apr 4		6th relieved the 10th Yorks & 1 Bn 1st Bde 4no two Coys in support as follows Map 51.B.S.W. :- Two front Coys T.17.b.5.3 to T.11.a.2.2 Supports in sunken road T.10.c T.6.5. T.12.a.c.	
	Apr 5th		7th Bn Leicestershire Regt moved Sudan Lights up to the left of Bn) preparing own Lewis gun & trench mortar & Lewis battery as indicators with 4.2" obsolute mortars to left at Bn.	
	Apr 6th		Situation & dispositions as on Apr 5th. Bn relieved at night by 8 Bn Leicestershire Regt. 8 casualties	
	Apr 7th		6th in rest at Hamelincourt. Bath - 2 hrs when gardens & resting time about 1 kilomtr N.W. of Bonville corner.	
	Apr 8th		6th at Hamelincourt. Bn ordered to move at 7.30 pm as agreed lunch & the orders of the 21st Bde. Battalion complete in rank left Hay St. Stan as a working party at T.9.2. by 4 pm.	

Army Form C. 2118.

WAR DIARY
or
INTELLIGENCE SUMMARY.
(Erase heading not required.)

Instructions regarding War Diaries and Intelligence Summaries are contained in F.S. Regs., Part II. and the Staff Manual respectively. Title pages will be prepared in manuscript.

Place	Date	Hour	Summary of Events and Information	Remarks and references to Appendices
	Apr 9th		Bn HQ & 2 Coys at Handsworth. The [illegible] at [illegible] R Bde [illegible] attack on a [illegible] position [illegible] at [illegible] 31.S.U	
	Apr 10		from T16.S.5 to T5.c.2.10 [illegible] 3 [illegible] After suffering casualties the two Coys retired [illegible] the front [illegible] of their line of work owing to a counter attack on S.W. 6 Hays Bde	
	Apr 11		Support from 60 Apr 10th [illegible] 28 Casualties reported from 0.9.17 to 14.4.17 to Apr 12th 60 Apr 10th [illegible] two [illegible] started out and retired to the [illegible] [illegible] to move on 9.S.S a.m. along the [illegible] side of Sun standing of me going to follow [illegible] [illegible] to be on Red side and sweeping. The [illegible] went up [illegible] not [illegible] at [illegible] no sign [illegible]	
			Rue two Coys were relieved by [illegible] Ly Bn and bus & [illegible] Bn to Hamelincourt. 36 Casualties.	
	Apr 14		B.HQ move to [illegible] at Moeuvres.	
	Apr 15		B.HQ moved to Ballecourt	
	Apr 23		B.HQ move to Cagnicourt	

WAR DIARY
or
INTELLIGENCE SUMMARY.
(Erase heading not required.)

Place	Date	Hour	Summary of Events and Information	Remarks and references to Appendices
	Ap. 24		B/M moved to Henincourt	
	" 25		B/M relieved 1.1.1 of Mayues from the Map 51B.S.W. T11c 2.2 to	
			T17 a 8.w.	
			Disposition the same except for a line of rifle pits held in rent Map 51B.SW	
	26-29		T5d T11b+d. Battl'n of companies by for in two	
	30		in rest at Bouline at Traou	

Approved 2/5/17
2nd Lieut Reg

WAR DIARY or INTELLIGENCE SUMMARY

Army Form C. 2118.

6th Leicester

Place	Date	Hour	Summary of Events and Information	Remarks and references to Appendices
BOISLEUX ST MARC	1/5/17		Reference Map 51 B S.W. Battalion at rest. Moved at night from HENINEL and relieved DLI Holding of the DLI in scattered trenches at N.35a.4.2.	
	2/5/17		Same dispositions. Making arrangements for attack on FONTAINES-LES-CROISILLES	
	3/5/17		Attack on FONTAINES-LES-CROISILLES. Operation unsuccessful	
	4/5/17		Battalion again at N.35a.4.2. Moved at night to assemble trenches at ---- reoccupying support posts at T.22d.5.2 T.22d.0.4 T.23c.9.9 T.28d.4.9 T.28.c.9.7	
	5/5/17 6/5/17 7/5/17		Dispositions as for Quiet days.	
	8/5/17		Battalion moved at 9 p.m. to relieve ---- at Saks GPs P.2 - P.23 ---- -----3 day a series of forward posts from 0.15c.2.8 to THQ P.2 7th Lincolnshire Regt on left 2/5th Yorks on right	
	9/5/17 10/5/17		Same dispositions Quiet day.	
	11/5/17		Battalion relieved at night by the 2nd Warwicks & marched to the main ? back at T.27.a.4.9.	

21/110

6th Bn Leic Regt (B) 6th Bn Leicester Regt

Vol F 22

WAR DIARY
or
INTELLIGENCE SUMMARY

Army Form C. 2118.

Place	Date	Hour	Summary of Events and Information	Remarks and references to Appendices
	12/5/17		Battalion moved at 10.30 AM & marched via MOYENVILLE & VETTES. Billets & MONCHI to rest billets at BERLES-AU-BOIS.	
BERLES AU BOIS	13/5/17 – 31/5/17		In rest at BERLES-AU-BOIS. In rest at BERLES-AU-BOIS. Training in Musketry and Tactical Schemes in the open. Effective Strength officers 35 O.R. 786.	174th Infy Bde. 6th Leicester Regt.

MAY 3rd. 1917.

Action at FONTAINES-LES-CROISILLES.

The 6th Leicestershire Regt was ordered to act in support to the two assaulting battalions, 8th & 9th Leicestershire Regt.

It was decided to support each battalion with 2 companies A & C on right B & D on left, the boundary between them as in the case of the leading battalions being ROTTON ROW.

The chief duty assigned to B Coy on the left was to take over from the 9th battalion, consolidate & hold the defensive flank covering N & W of FONTAINE WOOD.

Battalion Head Quarters were established at N36.c.3.4. those of the 8th battalion being in the same place.

Operations on right of ROTTON ROW. a wounded man of the 8th Battalion having reported that his battalion had reached the 1st objective A Coy advanced at 5.20.A.M. and keeping in touch with the HINDENBURG LINE reached a deep trench at T.6.b.1.2 in which were two platoons of the 8th Battalion. This company with the two platoons of the 8th Battalion advanced soon afterwards via the HINDENBURG LINE to a trench running from T.6.d.5.8. to U.1.b.1.7 On arrival in this latter trench connection was established with C Coy on left and D.L.I. on right.

C Coy then worked across the open on the left of A & occupied the same trench with a platoon in advance at U.1.a.2.6. which was held up in shell holes by heavy M.G. fire.

An attempt to bomb down BUSH TRENCH failed.

The trench up to U.1.b.4.5. was consolidated & at dusk the advanced platoon fell back into it.

A & C companies held this position until relieved.

Operations on the left of ROTTON ROW. The O.C. B Coy being killed & O.C. D Coy wounded it is difficult to obtain a reliable & narrative of events more especially as on this flank there was considerable confusion owing to the withdrawal across the front of troops of 18th Division.

Companies were ordered to advance at 5.10.A.M. B Coy advanced to a position at about O.31.d.9.1 when they were held up by M.G. fire & after making two lengths of trench remained in this position until relieved.

D Coy left about 150 yards in rear of B but were held up by M.G. fire from flanks & from a trench about 200 yards in front of RIVER ROAD.

They established posts at O.31.d.8.2, U.1.b.5.7 (in ROTTON ROW) U.1.b.5.5 with L.G. U.1.b.7.8 (in WOOD TRENCH) & V.1.a.9.2. These posts with the exception of the one in WOOD TRENCH were held until the Coy was relieved.

21/110

Army Form C. 2118.

WAR DIARY
INTELLIGENCE SUMMARY
(Erase heading not required.)

Place	Date	Hour	Summary of Events and Information	Remarks and references to Appendices
BERLES-AU-BOIS	1/6/17		Battn. in rest at BERLES-AU-BOIS. Monchy, Douchy, Ayettes.	
MOYENVILLE	2/6/17		Two companies (A & B) en route command of Capt McCoy move to sunken road at T22.c.4.8 to work under the direction of the R.E.'s on digging communication trenches.	
MOYENVILLE	3/6/17 4/6/17 5/6/17 6/6/17		As for 2/6/17 as before. Companies remaining at MOYENVILLE work on building & improving the camp.	
MOYENVILLE	7/6/17		Lt Col Stewart D.S.O. takes over command of the Battn. Battn. moved at 1.30 pm to Reserve Position behind CROISILLES. Dispositions as follow:- Battn H.Q. T.23.d.5.9 "A" Coy sunken road from T23.a.2.6 to T23.a.9.5 "B" " sunken road from T22.a.3.3 to T21.c.8.1 + Posts 4 & 5 "C" " trench from T23.d.4.5 to T23.c.75.75 "D" " trench from T23.c.75.75 to T23.a.2.1	

WAR DIARY
or
INTELLIGENCE SUMMARY

(Erase heading not required.)

Army Form C. 2118.

Place	Date	Hour	Summary of Events and Information	Remarks and references to Appendices
CROISILLES	8/6/17		Bn. relieves the same	
"	9/6/17		Uneventful day.	
"	10/6/17			
	11/6/17		Bn. moved up to the front line & took over a new sub sector from PLUM TRENCH (inclusive) to the SENSEE RIVER (exclusive) Dispositions were as follows:-	
			(a) Bn. H.Q. at T.18.b.8.1	
			(b) "A" Coy held HUMBER TRENCH and FORD TRENCH from PLUM LANE (inclusive)	
			(c) "B" Coy held HUMBER TRENCH and FORD TRENCH from 300 TRENCH (exclusive) to LUMP LANE (exclusive)	
			(d) "C" Coy held LUMP LANE from ROAD JUNCTION (TOWN TRENCH) U.7.b.50.25	
			(e) "D" Coy held River posts at U.7.b.8.7, U.7.b.1.6 and U.7.a.9.5	

WAR DIARY or INTELLIGENCE SUMMARY

Army Form C. 2118.

Map Ref 51B S.W.

Place	Date	Hour	Summary of Events and Information	Remarks and references to Appendices
CROISILLES	12/6/17		Dispositions the same	
	13/6/17		Uneventful days except for fairly heavy shelling	
	14/6/17			
	15/6/17			
	16/6/17		Bn. ordered to co-operate with the 131st Northumberland Fusiliers in an attack on TUNNEL TRENCH. The attack was held up and original dispositions maintained.	
	17/6/17		Dispositions the same.	
	18/6/17		Bn. H.Q. heavily shelled on the morning of the 17th inst.	
	19/6/17		Two companies relieved by the 5th B. Leicestershire Regt at dawn. The remaining two companies left the line at 10 p.m. & rejoined the remainder of the Bn. in "C" Camp at MOYENVILLE.	

Army Form C. 2118.

WAR DIARY
or
INTELLIGENCE SUMMARY

(Erase heading not required.)

Place	Date	Hour	Summary of Events and Information	Remarks and references to Appendices
MOYENVILLE	20/6/17		Batn. arrived at 11.30 a.m. & camp at HENDECOURT-LES-RANSART. Lt Col Attwood left the Battn. for Employ with Commandant of 110th Infantry Brigade. Major P.R. Yalland took command of the Batt.	
HENDECOURT LES RANSART	21/6/17 to 30/6/17		Battn. in rest at HENDECOURT-LES-RANSART. Training. Field firing. Musketry.	

E Yalland Major
Officer Commanding
O.R. 768.

Army Form C. 2118.

Maj u/ 51 B.Sw

WAR DIARY PALM. July 1917.
or
INTELLIGENCE SUMMARY.

(Erase heading not required.)

Place	Date July	Hour	Summary of Events and Information	Remarks and references to Appendices
HENDECOURT	1st		B'tn in rest. Moved at 6.30 AM and relieved the 2nd Worcestrs in C Camp at MOYENVILLE.	
MOYENVILLE	2		B'tn in Brigade Reserve. Lt Col Stewart D.S.O rejoined the B'tn from the 110th Inf Bde & took command	
	3		B'tn in Brigade Reserve	
	4		Training & Sports.	
MOYENVILLE	5			
	6			
	7			
MOYENVILLE	8		B'tn moved at 12 noon via ST LEGER & CROISILLES & relieved the 10th B'n ROYAL in the front line.	
			B'tn boundaries, from CURRANT LANE exclusive on the right to the SENSEE RIVER exclusive on the left	
			Coy distribution.	
			A Coy from CURRANT LANE (exclusive) to PEAR LANE exclusive	
			B " " PEAR LANE (inclusive) to LUMP LANE "	
			C " in LUMP LANE	
			D " in HIND TRENCH from LUMP LANE (exclusive) to SENSEE RIVER (exclusive) with forward NIGHT POST at junction of SHAFT TRENCH & SENSEE RIVER	

Army Form C. 2118.

WAR DIARY PALM
or
INTELLIGENCE SUMMARY.
(Erase heading not required.)

Place	Date July	Hour	Summary of Events and Information	Remarks and references to Appendices
CROISILLES.	9		Preparing the same.	
"	10		Uneventful days except for the shelling of	
"	11		the NEBO & LUMP LANE by the enemy.	
"	12			
"	13			
"	14		Bn. relieved at 12 noon by the 6th Bn Lee Regt. moved to Bn Reserve	
			Bn H.Q. T.22.d.5.9. sunken road	
			A Coy. T.17.c.8.2. "	
			B.C.O Sops. T.22 a & b "	
			In case of attack	
			Bn H.Q remained in same position	
			B Coy occupied VPs 1.2.3 & Railway & C line of posts	
			D " " 4 & 5 " " "	
			A " await orders	
			C moved to occupy the trenches of support to N at T 23 c.	
"	15			
	16		Preparing the same.	
	17			
	18			
	19		Finding working parties etc.	

21/1/110

Army Form C. 2118.

WAR DIARY
or
INTELLIGENCE SUMMARY.
(Erase heading not required.)

6th Bn Leicestershire Regt

Part of 91 B.S.N

Vol 24

Place	Date July	Hour	Summary of Events and Information	Remarks and references to Appendices
CROISILLES	20		B⁴⁰ moved at 8am & relieved the 6th Bn Leic Regt in the front line & took up the same dispositions & boundaries as in the 8th June.	
"	21		Dispositions the same, uneventful day.	
	22		Enemy blew a small mine under the MEDEA – LUMP LANE	
	23		Uneventful day. Dispositions the same	
	24		} Uneventful days. Dispositions the same.	
	25			
	26		B⁴⁰ relieved, relief starting at 3pm by 8th Bn Leic Regt & moved to Bde Reserve taking up the same dispositions as on July 14th.	
	27		⎫ Same dispositions.	
	28		⎪ Finding working parties etc.	
	29		⎬	
	30		⎪	
	31		⎭	

Effective strength 39 Officers 751 Other ranks.

W.R. Stewart Lt Col
Comdg 6th Leicester Regt

WAR DIARY or INTELLIGENCE SUMMARY.

Army Form C. 2118.

(Erase heading not required.)

21/ 6th Leic. Regt.
110th Inf. Bde
6th Leicester Regt.

Vol 23

252
3 sheet

Place	Date	Hour	Summary of Events and Information	Remarks and references to Appendices
CROISILLES	1/8/17		Bn relieved by 9th Royals & marched to C. Camp MOYENNEVILLE. Bn's arrived march 9am & strength 26 officers & marching ranks 740 with tanks	
MOYENNEVILLE	2/8/17 3/8/17 4/8/17 5/8/17 6/8/17		Training at MOYENNEVILLE	
	7/8/17		10 Brigade Field Day	
	8/8/17		Rest at MOYENNEVILLE	
MOYENNEVILLE	9/8/17		Bn relieved the 1st Lincolns in M.T. of the following dispositions. At 11am a working pty in St. LEGER & CROISILLES. Bn moved 6.30 am on frontage NELLY AVENUE (inclusive) to HIND ST North South [illegible]
B Coy - NORTH AVE N.E (inclusive) to PLUM LANE (inclusive)
A Coy - PLUM LANE (exclusive) to LUMP LANE (exclusive)
C Coy - LUMP LANE
D Coy - HIND TRENCH AND LUMP LANE (incl) to [illegible] AVE (incl)
[illegible] starting time [illegible] is that [illegible]
to the SE & SW [illegible]
10th & 8th Royals on right 7th & 8th Leic Regts on left	

Army Form C. 2118.

WAR DIARY
or
INTELLIGENCE SUMMARY.
(Erase heading not required.)

Instructions regarding War Diaries and Intelligence Summaries are contained in F. S. Regs., Part II. and the Staff Manual respectively. Title pages will be prepared in manuscript.

Place	Date	Hour	Summary of Events and Information	Remarks and references to Appendices
CROISILLES	10/8/17		Two coy's arrived of the 6th Bn Lincolnshire Regt. Supply parties detailed for work on CRAGSIDE TRENCH and LUMP LANE	
"	11/8/17 12/8/17 13/8/17		Same dispositions. Weather fine & dry.	
"	14/8/17		Bombardment of enemy trenches by heavy & medium Trench Mortars & Artillery	
"	15/8/17		Enemy obs posts near the MERS in BULLECOURT destroyed by our Artillery bombardment.	
"	16/8/17		Same dispositions. Weather fine & dry.	
"	17/8/17		Bombarded by 5.9" Jerho Shell took fire at 4 PM. Bn marched to CROISILLES - LEGLES HARDECOURT - X Road in 7 B 3 c	
HAMELINCOURT	18/8/17 19/8/17 20/8/17 21/8/17 22/8/17		Training in Camp a HAMELINCOURT	

Army Form C. 2118.

WAR DIARY
or
INTELLIGENCE SUMMARY.
(Erase heading not required.)

Instructions regarding War Diaries and Intelligence Summaries are contained in F. S. Regs., Part II. and the Staff Manual respectively. Title pages will be prepared in manuscript.

Place	Date	Hour	Summary of Events and Information	Remarks and references to Appendices
HAMELINCOURT	23/8/17		Bn moved to A Boisleux-au-Mont	
"	24/8/17		Training	
"	25/8/17		Bn marched via RANSART, BAILLEUL & GOUY-EN-ARTOIS to	
GOUY-EN-ARTOIS	26/8/17		Bn marched to MANIN & environs	
MANIN	27/8/17			
"	31/8/17		Training at MANIN	

Offrs 23
O/R 641

Army Form C. 2118.

WAR DIARY
INTELLIGENCE SUMMARY.
(Erase heading not required.)

6th Bn. Leicestershire Regt.

Place	Date	Hour	Summary of Events and Information	Remarks and references to Appendices
Meren	1.9.17 to 8.9.17		Battalion and Company training. Beautiful weather all week. Sports enjoyable for Officers and men.	
"	9.9.17		Church Parade	
"	10.9.17		Brigade Military Tournament. They won the most important event. The Company in the attack. Many other prizes were won including the Tug of War. WM Stewart. Weather glorious.	
"	11.9.17		Weather hot though in the afternoon the Officers attended an Army Gas Inhalation given by the Divisional Gas Officer. The remainder of the Battalion paraded en masse in the RSM and BSMs any time for a route march. WOs enjoyed it.	
"	12.9.17		Brigade Field Day. Weather damp, muddy and cold first. Army and Bgd Reserve carrying parties. The also extricate Platoon 6th Batt and for the first time in the Brigade. Very exciting tactics used of Aeroplane contact were appealing.	
"	13.9.17		Quiet day. Strong Advance party proceeded to CAESTRE to arrange billets.	
"	14.9.17		Battalion marched from MERIS to SAVY, starting at 2.a.m. got cleared at SAVY, arriving at CAESTRE and detraining at 10.30am. Billets rather 1 company billets being very scatteed.	
CAESTRE	14-22 9/17		Weather fine, some multiple training was carried out during these days.	

Army Form C. 2118.

WAR DIARY
or
INTELLIGENCE SUMMARY.

(Erase heading not required.)

Instructions regarding War Diaries and Intelligence Summaries are contained in F. S. Regs., Part II. and the Staff Manual respectively. Title pages will be prepared in manuscript.

Place	Date	Hour	Summary of Events and Information	Remarks and references to Appendices
CAESTRE	23.9.17		Paraded at 6.30 am and marched to FONTAINE HOUSE and about 10 am Pickets were placed over all areas during en route. May & Galland went forward in advance. Frosty weather. Fine	
FONTAINE HOUSE	24/9/17		Training. Lectures on the scenery by Kong and Lt Col S Ferris of the Brigade in camp for everyone.	
"	25/9/17		Training. Brig. Genl Chalmers spoke to the Officers. General during the afternoon at 5 pm.	
"	26/9/17		Exercise 30 N. Batt. (entrained) at FONTAINE HOUSE at 6.30 am proceeded to a dump (on the map) between LA CLYTTE and DICKEBUSCH. Packs were dumped at that point and the Battalion marched off at once to SCOTTISH WOOD. A Picket party (remainder of the Battn) Battalion in Corps Reserve - Battalion moved up to BEDFORD HOUSE at 7 pm.	
BEDFORD HOUSE (N.B. PICKET)	27/9/17		Quiet day. Batt. relieved by (4th & 6th Lond and formed 6 Coys at NICJ (Sheet 28 Belge-France)	
MICMAC CAMP	28/9/17		Weather still fine. Visited by X Corps Commander.	
NR DICKE-BUSCH	29/9/17		Bn moved on morning up to 6 camp of SCOTTISH WOOD H.35 d 6.8 Sheet 28 Belge-France.	
"	30/9/17		Bn moved up to the line and took over from 20 Bn 2 PM. Australian Infantry Brigade, on the YPRES-MENIN ROAD near HOOGE	

WAR DIARY
6th Bn. O'Leicestershire Regt
INTELLIGENCE SUMMARY
(Erase heading not required.)

Army Form C. 2118.

Place	Date	Hour	Summary of Events and Information	Remarks and references to Appendices
In the Field	1st Oct		Brigade Holding Line. 6th Bn. in Reserve in POLYGON WOOD. The following Officers & OR's were reported wounded in action. 2/Lt F.G. MOUNTFORD. 2/Lt A.F. WATSON. 2/Lt A.T. FARMER. 2/Lt H.S. WILDIN. 2/Lt G. LANE-ROBERTS the two latter remaining at duty.	
"	2nd Oct	Evening	The Batt. was relieved by the 3/4 Queens & moved to Camp in Scottish Wood. The following casualties were reported. Other ranks Killed Four. Wounded Eighty One.	
"	3rd Oct		Cleaned up & made preparations for returning to the line.	
"	4th Oct	8 am	Moved up to ZILLEBEKE Lake in Reserve to the 62nd Brigade.	
		6 pm	Moved up & concentrated in front of POLYGON WOOD. The following Officers & their reported KILLED in Action. 2/Lt W. KING PIGOTT (England) 2/Lt B.A. BASFORD. 2/Lt C.S. MARTIN. and Lieut Colin PHILBO. weather fair.	
"	5th Oct		In the evening we moved into the Front Line & relieved the 62nd Brigade occupying the Line from REUTEL to JOLTING HOUSES.	
"	6th Oct		Quiet day. No orguered. Rain at times.	
			Intermittent shelling during the day.	
	7th Oct	5.20 pm	Enemy put down a heavy barrage which lasted till 7 pm. No attack followed. Our Casualties were not heavy.	
	8th Oct	7 pm	Batt. was relieved by the 1st Royal Welsh Fusiliers. Arrived during the early hours of the morning and the RAILWAY EMBANKMENT ZILLEBEKE. 3 pm. We move from this place to encampment in SCOTTISH WOOD.	

Army Form C. 2118.

WAR DIARY
INTELLIGENCE SUMMARY.
(Erase heading not required.)

Place	Date	Hour	Summary of Events and Information	Remarks and references to Appendices
In the Field	9th Oct	2 pm	Moved from SCOTTISH WOOD to OUDERDOM and entrained for EBBLINGHEM arriving about 9.30 pm, and were billeted in the BLARINGHEM Area. The Transport moved by road.	
	10th		Day spent in cleaning up & reorganizing Platoons &c.	
	11th		Entrained back to SCOTTISH WOOD. Transport moved by road. See annex. A Coy were attached. 2/Lt N.S. HOGARTH moved to ENGLAND on leave. Seven other Ranks were reported to have died of Wounds received between 1st & 5th inst. 2/Lt T.S. DAVY reported Wm A on 4th inst. & Eleven Other Ranks reported killed between 5-7 inst.	
	12th		Day spent in cleaning up, stocktaking, Camp & Workshops to render more useful. Capt. J.W. BURDETT reported to the D.A.D. 4/10/17 & is missed at duty.	
	13th		1 Company operating in two of the 9th Training Coy Pl. 3 Coys Ranks (carrying parties) finding parties & instruction of the C.E. & Apps.	
	14th		— do —	
	15th		— do —	
	16th		— do —	
	17th		— — —	Capt. G.C.A. COX proceed to ENGLAND on leave.
	18th		— — —	
	19th		— — —	
	20th		— — —	
	21st		— — —	
	22nd		Moved from Camp in SCOTTISH WOOD to a Camp at H.25. a.6.7. (Sheet 23) Camp in a shocking condition — an absolute quagmire.	
	23rd		2/Lt Davy proceed on leave	

Army Form C. 2118.

WAR DIARY
INTELLIGENCE SUMMARY.
(Erase heading not required.)

Instructions regarding War Diaries and Intelligence Summaries are contained in F. S. Regs., Part II. and the Staff Manual respectively. Title pages will be prepared in manuscript.

Place	Date	Hour	Summary of Events and Information	Remarks and references to Appendices
In the Field	Oct 24th		General clean up. Overhaul of kit & preparation for future moves.	
	25th		Battn. Parade. Brigadier Genl. Lord Cocke, C.M.G., D.S.O. presented ribbons & medals for gallantry in the field to Pte. Nage & Tyer.	
			Day spent in general improvement of camp, laying trench boards & relieving drainage through the mud. 2/Lt. Briance to England on leave.	
	26th		Very wet day. Work impossible, camp badly flooded.	
	27th		Day spent in organisation of Battn. ready for moving into the line.	
	28th	2 p.m.	Battn. moved into reserve, Railway Embankment, Zillebeke.	
	29th	2-30 p.m.	Battn. moved up into supports, relieving the 8th Bn. 2/(Sept) Rif. Bn. at CRAPPIT JUNCTION & 2 Coys (A+B) in close supports in POLYGON Wood.	
	30th		Still in Support. Casualties reported. Other Ranks. Killed one. Wounded, eleven.	
	31st		The Battn. moved into the Front line at REUTEL relieving 7th B.W. Ten Other Ranks reported wounded.	
			Total Casualties for the month. Killed in Action Officers 2. Other Ranks 24. Died of wounds R.O. in Action. Officers nil. O.Rs. 12. Wounded, Officers 7. Other Ranks 169. Missing 3.	

[signature]

6th Lincolns Regt 1/11

WAR DIARY or INTELLIGENCE SUMMARY

Army Form C. 2118.

282
7 sheets

Place	Date	Hour	Summary of Events and Information	Remarks and references to Appendices
	Nov 1st		Walker Fine. Day fairly quiet except for occasional bursts of hostile artillery fire. Casualties:- No.10517 Pte COTTON E.V. } 20154 " BENNETT S. } Wounded. 20125 " SMITH H. 242592 " ARMSDEN H. } Gassed. Lt. J.H. SMEDLEY proceeded on leave to England.	
	2nd		Heavy shelling during the night. Weather fine. Casualties:- 2nd Lt. H. JOHNSON 2nd Lt. H.A. LEE } Wounded 2nd Lt. H.E. MAYFIELD 2nd Lt for unnamed at duty No.10408 Sgt DUDLEY A 40022 Lce/Cpl DOLLEY A } Killed in action 40320 Pte EASTON W. 20973 " KNOTT R. 201192 " ATKINS W } died of wounds 22182 " MARSH A } killed in action No.291102 Pte GEARY W.A } Gassed 25395 " CHANDLER J 404115 " ASTELL L } Wounded 15157 " GRANT J 201790 " LEE C 21853 " WRIGHT E 33141 " TOMPKINS F * on duty	
	3rd		Fine weather and a quiet day. Troubles in a fairly good condition. Casualties:- 201192 Pte ATKINS } died of wounds 33274 " SIBLEY E.W. } Gassed 34015 " EATON W. } Wounded	

WAR DIARY or INTELLIGENCE SUMMARY.

Army Form C. 2118.

Place	Date	Hour	Summary of Events and Information	Remarks and references to Appendices
	Nov 4th		An intense enemy barrage put on our lines in the early morning, otherwise a quiet day. Batt. was relieved at night by the 3/4th Royal West Surrey Rt (Queens) and proceeded to ZILLEBEKE LAKE. Casualties:- Lt F.W. Curtis Killed 21196 Pte Johnson C. " 203341 " Harris H.) in 331554 " Keech G.) action 30833 " Parsons F.E.) Bruised	
	5th		The Batt. marched to BREWERY CAMP, DICKEBUSCH No 11155 Pte Cashbolt J. reported missing	Sheet 28 H 25 D
	6th		Day in camp. Spent in cleaning up + reorganising the men. Weather cold & damp.	
	7th		Maj: Gen: D Campbell decorates Capt G.C.A. Cox and Capt J.B. Garner with the Military Cross.	

WAR DIARY
or
INTELLIGENCE SUMMARY.

Army Form C. 2118.

Place	Date	Hour	Summary of Events and Information	Remarks and references to Appendices
	Nov 7th (Sun)		and the following with Military Medals:— 33302 Sgt. JACKSON S. 16207 Cpl. PRATT.? 10183 Sgt. HAWKINS C.H. 25746 Sgt. DOWNS T. 21879 Pte. MALCOLM P. 16224 Sgt. DENNIS C.K. 20461 " WARREN W. 20195 Pte. SOUTER Q. 7974 Sgt. ROBERTS G 20344 " COX W. 21180 Pte. GIBBS G 33018 " BUNYAN H	
	8th		Batt. still at DICKEBUSCH, and preparing for another tour in the Line. Lt.-Col. W.N. Stewart D.S.O. proceeded on leave to England.	
	9th	3.15 p.m.	The Batt. marched to RAILWAY DUGOUTS, ZILLEBEKE and arrived there about 5 p.m. H.Q. and A.C. and D Coys relieved the 10th K.O.Y.L.I. & we are Company. B Coy went straight on & relieved one Company 10th KOYLI at the BUTTE DE POLYGONE	BELGIUM FRANCE SHEET 28
	10th		At ZILLEBEKE in reserve	
	11th		The Batt. proceeded to relieve the 7th Bn. Lincolnshire Regt in the front line	

WAR DIARY
or
INTELLIGENCE SUMMARY.

(Erase heading not required.)

Army Form C. 2118.

Place	Date	Hour	Summary of Events and Information	Remarks and references to Appendices
	Nov 11th (cts)		Hostile artillery quiet on the way up & Batt. arrived at the front line at 8.30 pm Dispositions: "D" Coy on the right (J 6 B. 30. 35 to J 5 D 75.85) "A" " " left (J 5 B) "C" " in support (J 5 Central) "D" " in reserve (J 4 D 9.5) Batt. H.Q at J 5.C.15.80.	Part of Sout 28 BECELAERE
	12th		Quiet day in the front line, but outpost & reserve positions were intermittently shelled all day. Casualties - 34424 Pte GOULD C.W. wounded Enemy aircraft very active, flying at extraordinarily low altitudes. 25919 " DIXEY F.J wounded	
	13th		A quiet day again and near lines shelled as yesterday. Casualties - 32959 L/C STEARN C. } Killed in action 11535 Pte HIND S.J 32547 " SMITH W.H } Wounded 21180 " GIBBS G.H 40337 " MAGIN A	
	14th		Conditions the same as the two previous days. The Batt. was relieved during the evening by 3rd Auckland Batt. N.Z.R. & then proceeded to RAILWAY DUGOUTS ZILLEBEKE. Hostile artillery was fairly active on the back area. Casualties - Lt J.H WYATT wounded No Hotel Pte YALE W.H accidentally killed 40527 " GRAINGER A. wounded	

Army Form C. 2118.

WAR DIARY
or
INTELLIGENCE SUMMARY.
(Erase heading not required.)

Place	Date	Hour	Summary of Events and Information	Remarks and references to Appendices
	Nov 15th		Batt: at ZILLEBEKE. Spent the day fixing to remove so much mud as possible from own clothing, cleaning up generally. In response to A.R. N.Z. I. Bde No 29555 Pte SACOFSKY reported missing whereas killed. 2/Lt C. Osborne joined this Batt.	Sheet 28 Ypres
	16th		Batt. proceeded to SCOTTISH WOOD & relieved 3rd CANTERBURY REGIMENT. Billeted in huts.	Sheet 28A
	17th		Batt. marched to RENINGHELST, and billeted there for the night.	
	18th		The Batt. proceeded to LE CHIEN BLANC. Had dinner en route and arrived in billets about 4 pm. Lt F.S. Scholes proceeded on leave to England.	
	19th		Batt. marched to NEUF BERQUIN.	
	20th		Batt. marched to ANNEZIN.	LENS 11
	21st		Batt. marched to COUPIGNY. Billeted in huts.	
	22nd		At COUPIGNY. Village shelled during the day.	LENS 11

WAR DIARY or INTELLIGENCE SUMMARY

Army Form C. 2118.

Place	Date	Hour	Summary of Events and Information	Remarks and references to Appendices
	Nov 23rd		Batt: at COUPIGNY. Village again shelled intermittently during the day & night. Major Genl. A CAMPBELL awarded his Cards of Honour to:- Lt H.S. WILDIN " T.S. DAVY 2/Lt H.S. DAVIS No. 33302 C.S.M. JACKSON S. " 16>>24 Sgt DENNIS T.H. " 16207 Cpl PRATT C. " 10982 Pte THORNTON T. " 12506 " HARRISON G. " 25344 " COX W. " 10182> " LOWE D. " 16294 " ENSOR R. " 37992 " WYKES E. " 2180 " GIBBS G.H. " 20644 " WARREN A. " 10879 " CLARKE F. 10145 Pte JOHNSON H.R. 2879 " MALKIN P. 10185 Sgt HAWKINS H. 17774 Sgt ROBERTS G. 30644 L/C WEBSTER J.A. 10706 Pte KNIGHT G. 20145 " SOUTER G. 32618 " COPE J.H. 14424 " BRIGGS F. 46357 " MAGIN H.T. 16317 " HUDSON H. 25746 " DOWNES T. 11167 " FOSTER A. 33032 " BUNYAN H. The following letter was received from G.O.C. X'th Corps:- "On your departure from X'th Corps I wish to thank you for all your great & excellent work &c. of which my command. In parting from you which I do with regret I wish you all good luck for the future"	Refs Map 36B
At COUPIGNY	24th		1. Q.M. W.J.GREEN proceeded on leave to England. 2/Lt H.T. 140.R arrived at the Batt.	
	25th		The Batt marched to MONCHY-BRETON. The Commanding Officer, Company Commanders & Intelligence Officer proceeded by Lorry to ROCLINCOURT & reconnoitred the line around OPPY.	
	26th		Batt. at MONCHY-BRETON, carrying on training.	

WAR DIARY
or
~~INTELLIGENCE~~ **SUMMARY.**
(Erase heading not required.)

Army Form C. 2118.

Place	Date	Hour	Summary of Events and Information	Remarks and references to Appendices
At MONCHY - BRETON.	Nov 27th		A draft of 84 O.R. arrived at the Batt.	
	28th		Training. Lt-Col: W.N. STEWART represented the Divisional into of honours to Officers of the Batt: mentioned in his diary of 23rd Nov. A draft of 31 O.R. arrived at the Batt. The following Officers reported for duty: 2/Lt. H.J.S. DIXON	
	29th		The Batt. spent the day in the Lewis training. Orders received that the Batt: would probably move from this area to-morrow to the CHELERS area. 2/Lt H.T. FROMER rejoined the Batt. from Hospital.	
	30th		Sudden orders received at 4.30 p.m. that the Batt. was to march to SAVY & entrain there at 6 p.m. The train moved off about midnight & arrived at TINCOURT at 10 A.M. on the 1st December.	Ref. Map LENS II Ref. Map 62 C

R. Rumsey
Adj. 6. Lec. Regt.

WAR DIARY
INTELLIGENCE SUMMARY
(Erase heading not required.)

Army Form C. 2118.

6th [eventh?] Regt

Dec 1917

Place	Date 1917	Hour	Summary of Events and Information	Remarks and references to Appendices
TINCOURT	DEC 1st		Arrived TINCOURT (G.C.) at 10a.m. No knowledge when we were going, but with rumours of enemy counter attacks, &c. Marched to BUIRE and billeted in huts.	
VILLERS-FAUCON	2nd		Moved by march route to VILLERS-FAUCON.	
do.	3rd		In huts at VILLERS-FAUCON. Battalion standing to "between dawn and sun set."	
EPEHY	4th		6th Battalion relieved 7th Batt in left subsector in front of 84th Bde. "C" Coy on right, "D" Coy on left, "A" Coy in close support, "B" Coy in Reserve trench.	
			CASUALTIES.	
			No. 7974 Sgt ROBERTS. G. (at duty) WOUNDED	
			" 40006 Cpl BASSON. E.T. "	
			" 10874 LCpl WALT HO. H. "	
			" 32992 Pte WYKES. E. "	
			" 11578 " JENNINGS. C. "	
EPEHY	5th		Very quiet day in the line. Battalion takes over one coy front from 9th K.O.Y.L.I.	
EPEHY	6th		CASUALTIES.	
			No 21099 Pte HARROLD J.H. WOUNDED	
			" 20586 " ALDRIDGE. T. "	
			" 38234 " GREEN. G. "	
			" 21739 " BORDOLI. B. "	

WAR DIARY
INTELLIGENCE SUMMARY

Army Form C. 2118.

Place	Date	Hour	Summary of Events and Information	Remarks and references to Appendices
EPEHY	Dec (cont)			
	7th		Enemy sent over a number of trench trap about 3 pm when the working parties were working. Quiet day in line.	
do	8th			
do	9th		Battalion relieved by 16 Rosters and went back to Reserve at Railway Embankment. Enemy shown front line between — FALLING TREE ROAD. Quiet day except at 2 pm a number of 10.2 & 95 field shells landing about an hour.	
do	10th		CASUALTIES	
			No. 10507 PTE. PIGG. J. WOUNDED " 32801 " BIDDLES. R " " 2/107 " HOLLAND. T.W " " 11933 SGT. ROWLAND. W " (at duty) Lt and QM. W.J. GREEN proceeded on leave to England.	
do	11th		Quiet day in line	
do	12th		Batn relieved 7th Letters in front line. New boundary between Batns approx from X 26a 87.70 — X 25b 8.3	
do	13th		CASUALTY. No. 40378 PTE. WYLES. W. KILLED. 2 Lt. C.T. LOVELL proceeded to England on leave.	
do	14th		Quiet day in line	

Army Form C. 2118.

WAR DIARY
INTELLIGENCE SUMMARY.
(Erase heading not required.)

Place	Date	Hour	Summary of Events and Information	Remarks and references to Appendices
EPEHY	15th		Front line withdrawn on the night 9/15/16th. Company & men	
			CAPT. LTS. NOBBS proceeded on leave to England.	
do	16th		Battn relieved by 6th Battn and concentrated at VILLERS FAUCON	
VILLERS-FAUCON	17th		Day occupied in cleaning up. A, B & C Coys in reserve trenches	
do	18th		C.O. addressed Corps.	
SAULCOURT	19th		Battn moved to huts at SAULCOURT	
			2/Lt E. GAUL proceeded on leave to England	
EPEHY	20th		Battn relieved 7th Battn in front line	
			2/Lt H.S. DAVIS proceeded on leave to England	
do	21st		Day very quiet. Occasional M.G. fire	
do	22nd		Very quiet day in line	
			2/Lt. T. L. THIRLBY proceeded on leave to England.	
do	23rd		Very quiet day in line	
do	24th		Battn relieved by 7th Battn. Battn then took up positions in	
			defence line of EPEHY, C and D Coys being billeted in village,	
			At B along the railway embankment.	
do	25th		CHRISTMAS DAY honor festivities postponed till we get out of line	
do	26th		Day very quiet. Each Coy in present position "stand to" from 6 to 9	

WAR DIARY or INTELLIGENCE SUMMARY.

Army Form C. 2118.

(Erase heading not required.)

Place	Date	Hour	Summary of Events and Information	Remarks and references to Appendices
EPEHY	27th		CAPT. J.P. THIERENS proceeded on leave to England.	
EPEHY	28th		On the night of the 28th/29th the 6th Battn relieved the 7th Battn in the front line. Weather bitterly cold took drifting snow 4 ft of snow was found in the trenches.	
"	29th		A quiet day. Weather remained the same. Capt J.D. Farmer M.C. proceeded on leave.	
"	30th		No activity in the line. The Battalion experienced a little stiff earthquake. Trench Mortars during the tour owing to the extremely cold weather and trenches. 2nd. Lt. E.S. Hume-Roberts proceeded on leave.	
"	31st		Line very quiet. Weather remained bitterly cold with snow.	

Army Form C. 2118.

WAR DIARY
or
INTELLIGENCE SUMMARY.
(Erase heading not required.)

January 1918   6th Bn Leicestershire Regt   Vol 30

30 2 sheets

Instructions regarding War Diaries and Intelligence Summaries are contained in F. S. Regs., Part II. and the Staff Manual respectively. Title pages will be prepared in manuscript.

Place	Date 1918	Hour	Summary of Events and Information	Remarks and references to Appendices
EPEHY	January 1		The Battn was relieved from front line & returned to Bde Reserve at SAUCOURT. Weather still bitterly cold. The relief was well carried out without casualties. Major Br Lt Col (T/Lt Col) E.L. CHALLONER D.S.O promoted & appointed to the Most Distinguished order of St Michael & St George & to be additional member of 3rd Class & Companion B said order.	
SAUCOURT	2		Battn rested & cleaned up. Preparations were made for Xmas dinner to be held next day.	
"	3		Battn had their much delayed Xmas dinner which was a great success. Weather was bitterly cold with snow on the ground. 2/Lt FARMER proceeded on leave to UK.	
"	4		Battn moved from its old camp to a new & another better one about 400 x away No. 4 Bde became Divl Reserve. Lt Col W.N. STEWART, D.S.O returned to Battn after commanding Bde. B/Gen¹ D.E. CAILEY CMG took over 110th Bde from Lord LOCH who proceeded to U.K for operation.	
"	5		Weather bitterly cold. Bn still resting.	
"	6		Bn had to supply working parties for tunnelling & dugouts. Weather the same Lt Col W.N. STEWART D.S.O proceeded on leave to Paris	
"	7		Bn had to supply working parties for tunnelling & dugouts. Weather the same.	
"	8		Bn has to supply working parties for tunnelling & dugouts. Weather the same.	
"	9		Bn has to supply working parties for tunnelling & dugouts. Weather the same.	

WAR DIARY or INTELLIGENCE SUMMARY.

(Erase heading not required.)

Army Form C. 2118.

Place	Date 1918	Hour	Summary of Events and Information	Remarks and references to Appendices
SAULCOURT	Jany 10		Bn supplied working parties for tunnelling & dug outs & wiring.	
"	11		Bn supplied working parties for tunnelling dugouts & wiring. Lieut J.W. BURDETT proceeded to U.K. for 1 month's leave. Lt Col. W.N. STEWART. D.S.O. returned from PARIS.	
"	12		Bn supplied working parties as on 11th. Weather cold.	
"	13		Bn supplied working parties as on 11th. Weather cold.	
"	14		Bn supplied working parties as on 11th. Following officers joined Bn from Base. 2/Lt C.R. FALLAS 2/Lt J.W. SHOOTER (posted "C"Co) 2/Lt W.E. MAJOR (posted B Co)	
"	15		Bn supplied working parties for tunnelling & dug outs. Bn moved to new camp in LIERAMONT. Very bad camp. Weather very bad.	
LIERAMONT	16		Bn found fatigue parties Town. Major LONGRAVES & Lieut STROKE & Lieut STROKE proceeded on leave to U.K. Weather wet. 2/Lt P.J. STROKE proceeded on leave to U.K.	
"	17		Bn found fatigue parties as on 16th. Weather wet.	
"	18		Bn found fatigue parties as on 16th. Weather fine. Relieved by 2/6 Battn 1912. 9.00 Brigade at 2.30	
"	19		Bn found fatigue parties as on 16th. Weather wet.	
"	20		110" Bde relieved 64" Bde in front line. Bn relieved 9th A&S.H. in left sub sector "C" Coy At front line & Coy Railway Cutting & Coy. "D"Coy L front line & Co. Pby Cutting & Co. "B Coy Support line & Coy Pby Battery & Coy. "A"Co Reserve in Cutting. Installations lights wiring. 2nd Lt W. BOND atta to Bond attd D Trenches which had fallen in owing to the thaw. 2/Lt J.H. HARRATT proceeded on leave to U.K.	

Army Form C. 2118.

WAR DIARY
or
INTELLIGENCE SUMMARY.
(Erase heading not required.)

Instructions regarding War Diaries and Intelligence Summaries are contained in F. S. Regs., Part II. and the Staff Manual respectively. Title pages will be prepared in manuscript.

Place	Date 1918	Hour	Summary of Events and Information	Remarks and references to Appendices
EPEHY	Jany 21		Quiet day – Slight shelling. Weather fine	
"	22		Quiet day. Weather raining.	
"	23		Quiet day. Our aeroplane dropped a bomb in front 1 in front 1 D PLANE TRENCH. Major C.E.R. HOLROYD SMYTH M.C. joined Bn as Second in Command.	
"	24		Quiet day. Bn relieved by 7th Bn Fus Reg & moved to EPEHY. "B" Coy in village. "C" Coy in Rly Cutting, right of FALLEN TREE RD. "D" Coy in Reg wood in front B. During the first 24 hrs returned patrolling has been carried out. A silong [?] amount of Boche fast up in front 1 D PLANE TRENCH. Major J.C. BURDETT M.C. proceeded on leave to UK.	
"	25		Rest. No work. Weather fine. 2/Lt B.L. ASQUITH joined Batt'n. Posted B Coy.	
"	26		Work carried out by day on enlarging defences. Two parties of 60 ORs supplied to RE at night to work on front line. Weather misty.	
"	27		Quiet day. Work as for 26th. Capt. A MCLAY M.C. proceeded on leave to UK for 1 month. Weather misty.	
"	28		Work carried out on enlarge defences. Bn relieved 7th Bn Fus Reg in front line Reps sector. A Coy and platoon tons sect Rt Front line Support line 3 Platoons C Coy R Front line Left D Coy & Coy HQrs Support Lt Coy. B Coy L Front line & Coy Rly Cutting, & Coy A Coy in Reserve in Rly Cutting. Weather fine.	

Army Form C. 2118.

WAR DIARY
or
INTELLIGENCE SUMMARY.
(Erase heading not required.)

IV.

Instructions regarding War Diaries and Intelligence Summaries are contained in F.S. Regs., Part II. and the Staff Manual respectively. Title pages will be prepared in manuscript.

Place	Date 1918	Hour	Summary of Events and Information	Remarks and references to Appendices
EPEHY	Jany 29		Quiet day. Weather fine.	
"	30		Quiet day. Weather fine.	
"	31		Quiet day. Weather frosty. 2/Lt R.H. LORD proceeded on leave.	

SAULCOURT.
Feby 2nd/1918

W.N. Stewart. Lt Col
Comdg. 6th Br. Lincolnshire Regt

Army Form C. 2118.

WAR DIARY
or
INTELLIGENCE SUMMARY.
(Erase heading not required.)

6th LEICESTERSHIRE REGT.

Place	Date	Hour	Summary of Events and Information	Remarks and references to Appendices
EPEHY (Fresnoy)	1.2.17		10909 Sgt North N.G. awarded Belgian Croix de Guerre. Batt relieved by 7th Leicestershire Regt and proceeded to SAULCOURT Bde Reserve. Weather Frosty	
SAULCOURT	2.2.17		Transport moved to LIERAMONT. Batter Rest. Weather fine	
do	3.2.17		Rest. Batt took a special divine service & preparedness. Weather fine & bright.	
do	4.2.17		Batt relieved 7th Leic. Regt in Fresnoy. A Coy Right Batt. Centre hold Coy in Front and half in Support. D Coy in reserve. Weather fine	
EPEHY	5.2.17		Front very quiet. Owing to fine weather aircraft on both sides very active.	

Army Form C. 2118.

WAR DIARY
or
INTELLIGENCE SUMMARY.
(Erase heading not required.)

Instructions regarding War Diaries and Intelligence Summaries are contained in F. S. Regs., Part II. and the Staff Manual respectively. Title pages will be prepared in manuscript.

Place	Date	Hour	Summary of Events and Information	Remarks and references to Appendices
EPEHY	5.2.0		Enemy sent up regards over about ½ an hour out of tender fire. Weather fine	
do	7.2.17		20109/ Pte Howard H wounded by H.G. bullet. During this tour on the line Rubligines was generally quiet. The afternoon fire and my accurate aimed at. Enemy. Relieved by 7th Lan. R'ts and proceeded to Huts at H.W.S. by motor wagons and light railway. Weather fine	
HALT ALAINS	8.2.15		Baths. Reading and General cleaning up. Weather showery	
do	9.2.17		Battn reorganised into 4 Platoons per Coy incorporating Draft and some men from 9th Battn. Weather fine	
do	10.2.17		C Coy on range firing Lewis and Hotchkiss guns. Church Service Weather fine	

Army Form C. 2118.

WAR DIARY
or
INTELLIGENCE SUMMARY.
(Erase heading not required.)

Instructions regarding War Diaries and Intelligence Summaries are contained in F. S. Regs., Part II. and the Staff Manual respectively. Title pages will be prepared in manuscript.

Remarks and references to Appendices: 6 Leicestershire Regt Vol

Places	Date	Hour	Summary of Events and Information
HEM T A'LAINES	11.2.15		A&D Coy on 500x range. Lecture by Capt Thornton (Contrade Off) on Intelligence. Draft 3 Offr 60 ORs from 9th Battn. came. Weather fine
do	12.2.15		Training. Battn viewed at which Brig. Gen. Oakley Comd. of Trenches. Scents hosted for Soarers 21st Div Concert Party. Weather fine
do	13.2.15		
do	14.2.15		Move to Moislains (Don Camp) very dirty camp. Weather fine
MOISLAINS	15.2.15		Morning spent in cleaning up for C in C inspection. Battn inspected by Sir Douglas Haig. Transport turn on 500x range. Weather very cold & frosty.
do	16.2.15		Training. Battn passed through Gas Chamber. Weather cold & frosty
do	17.2.15		Church Parade. Work taken over on Green Line. Weather frosty

Army Form C. 2118.

WAR DIARY
or
INTELLIGENCE SUMMARY.
(Erase heading not required.)

Instructions regarding War Diaries and Intelligence Summaries are contained in F. S. Regs., Part II. and the Staff Manual respectively. Title pages will be prepared in manuscript.

Place	Date	Hour	Summary of Events and Information	Remarks and references to Appendices
HUISSANS	18.2.17		300 men working on Greenlines. Both moved ICARAMONT and kept men from 78 L.m.S. Coy. & 96 L.m.S. Coy. greatly improved for A.A defences. Weather cold	
WERAMONT	19.2.15		300 men working on Greenlines. One Coy training. Weather cold	
do	20.2.15		250 men working at QUINCEONCE. Improving lines by outposts	
			270 men working on Greenlines plus 3 coys 17.113. Weather cold	
do	21.2.15		300 men working on Greenlines. 240 working at QUINCEONCE. Weather very disagreeable	
do	22.2.15		270 men working on Greenlines. 250 at QUINCEONCE. Burying	
do	23.2.15		Working parties as on 22nd. Battn moved to SUYCOURT. Weather cold and showery	

Army Form C. 2118.

WAR DIARY
or
INTELLIGENCE SUMMARY.
(Erase heading not required.)

6th Leicestershire Regt

Place	Date	Hour	Summary of Events and Information	Remarks and references to Appendices
SAILLCOURT	24.2.18		4.50 all tents working on YELLOW LINE ENEMY Weather fine very warm	
do	25.2.18		Working parties as on 24th Weather very warm	
do	26.2.18		Working parties as on 24th Weather showery	
do	27.2.18		Working parties as on 24th & 5th Possible taking up position on BROWN LINE 6-0 P.M Weather fine very cold.	
do	28.2.18		Working parties as on 24th. Batt. reported notified of support of ENEMY Weather very cold.	

110th Inf.Bde.
21st Div.

WAR DIARY

6th BATTN. THE LEICESTERSHIRE REGIMENT.

M A R C H

1 9 1 8

WAR DIARY or **INTELLIGENCE SUMMARY**

Army Form C. 2118.

6 Leicesters 24/1/18

Place	Date	Hour	Summary of Events and Information	Remarks and references to Appendices
EPEHY	March 1		Jn Support EPEHY. Working on POSTS in EPEHY and YELLOW LINE.	
	2nd		—	
	3rd		—	
	4th		Night of 4/5th relieved 8th Bn Leicesters in front line. Coys in Regt Sect Sector. Very little work done in front line. Enemy unusually quiet, probably in pullage.	
	5th		FIRE SUPPORT and RED LINE.	
	6th		—	
	7th		—	
	8th		Night of 8/9th relieved 8th Bn Leicesters and went in Support to EPEHY. Work on POSTS in EPEHY and YELLOW LINE also daily party to working on pillbox defences under R.E. supervision.	
	9th			
	10th			
	11th			
	12th		Night of 12/13th relieved 8th Bn Leicesters in line in Right Sub Sect. No work done in front line, all available men working on FIRE SUPPORT and RED LINE.	
	13th			
	14th			
	15th		A raid was carried out by "C" Coy on enemy POST (X21d.10.95). (Ref Map 78o) It started at Zero, lifted onto Pillbox and 70 yds. Result 2 Boche killed & 1 prisoner taken, had Box barrage by artillery, excellent. Raid a great success.	
	16th		Congratulatory message from Bde & Cpt, Dimond & Bde Commander on a success ful raid & being Kaiser.	
			Relief delayed till night	

Army Form C. 2118.

WAR DIARY
or
INTELLIGENCE SUMMARY.
(Erase heading not required.)

Place	Date	Hour	Summary of Events and Information	Remarks and references to Appendices
EPEHY.	March 21		Night of 20/21st relieved 8th Bn Leicestershire Regt. in EPEHY.	
			"A" & "D" Coy with Capt McLean M.C. in EPEHY, in support of Posts and in Support of Company	
			"B" Coy in huts at SAULCOURT with "Battle Patrols" in YELLOW LINE	
			"C" Coy Counter-attacking Coy.	
			The 6th Bn Leicestershire Regt. in support.	
Orders for an "Battle Stations" ordered.	
			"A" & "D" Coys. Garrison Posts in EPEHY	
			"B" "C" Coy. Left SAULCOURT at dawn; a fair deal of hostile Artillery fire encountered	
			Getting into position through hostile barrage. H.E. & S.G.	
			In position in YELLOW LINE by 7.30 a.m. Heavy bombardment all along	
			the morning.	
11.45am	Enemy reported as breaking through 16th Div. on our right.	
		2.30pm	MALASSISE FARM reported to be held by the Germans.	
		3.35pm	MALASSISE FARM held by enemy. Enemy also in PINGSBY WOOD.	
			TETARD WOOD still in our hands.	
			16th M/G Holding strong point on RAILWAY EMBANKMENT.	
			5th S.G. Howitzer Battery near EPEHY at SAULCOURT ROAD within 3 feet,	
			abandoning one	
			Enemy seen advancing in force between MALASSISE FARM and	
			RONSSOY; appeared to be massing in SUNKEN ROAD	
			about this time stopping from 16th Div were coming back in small	
			parties.	
		4.45pm	Counter-attack with TANK carried out at our right in direction	
			of RONSSOY WOOD.	
		6 pm	It became necessary to form a defensive flank along ST EMILIE Rd	

Army Form C. 2118.

WAR DIARY
or
INTELLIGENCE SUMMARY.
(Erase heading not required.)

Place	Date	Hour	Summary of Events and Information	Remarks and references to Appendices
EPEHY.	March 24	6 pm	also to withdraw from FRONT LINE to CLOSE SUPPORT LINE: Enemy in our sight having nearly reached BROWN LINE.	
		7 pm to 9 am	YELLOW LINE heavily shelled; FRONT LINE pushed out altogether.	
		9 pm	Fairly quiet. Patrols sent out in front of our line, no sight of enemy.	
		6.30 am		
	22nd 6.30 am		Intense bombardment of FRONT LINE for over an hour, which extended to CLOSE SUPPORT LINE. Troubled by snipers in rear of YELLOW LINE. During the night 21/22nd Two Field Coys of Royal Engineers came up & one with our orders. One Coy from the Reserve Brigade & three pigeons. Here also to have come under our orders but failed to go so on account of being unable to get through hostile barrage.	
		8.40 am	About this time Lt Col Mr Stewart D.S.O. was killed. Men shot through the head by a sniper; death being instantaneous. Command of the Battalion being taken over by Major S.E. Burdett.	
		8.50 am	Enemy reported to be massing in front of YELLOW LINE: patrols being sent into regard of our line.	
		9 am	Enemy attempted to bomb down communication trench leading to our FRONT LINE, but were knocked out by a Lewis gun.	
		9.30 am	Enemy worked round both flanks & we were surrounded.	
		11 am	A serious action was fought in the BROWN LINE forming a defensive flank on the EPEHY – SAULCOURT road, Reserve Brig....	

WAR DIARY or INTELLIGENCE SUMMARY

Army Form C. 2118.

Place	Date	Hour	Summary of Events and Information	Remarks and references to Appendices
	Mar 22nd	11 am	HQ the 8/9th Leicestershire Regt. Enemy were now attacking N of ROCHE RIVER, tanks from the BROWN LINE. The TANKS checked the enemy advance by enfilading by Enemy in EQUAY - SAILLOURT ROAD. Also withdrew to FEROPOOMS - LONGAVESNES - 7th & 8th Rifle Brigade formed LONGAVESNES - SAULCOURT ROAD through BROWN LINE. NORTH of ENEMY - SAULCOURT to small groups. As enemy under heavy shelling a barrage for some time. CAPRON COPSE and SAULCOURT during afternoon. LONGAVESNES being shelled, with AER around Germans. MARCOURT - LE - HAUT. Nine (9) of the enemy tanks. About MIDDAY (?) Mc helped the tank officially destroy one ENEMY LINE. On the BROWN LINE of ERINETTE ROAD; FLIER who held until about	
	23rd	10 am	POSTON had taken up POSITION RD SOUTH of MARDO COPSE & HIS WITHDREW to MORSAINS - MIDINETTE LINE from his position his eventually taken up on high ground east of ALLAINES and	
	24th		CLERY till he was relieved with morning 1500/2000 yards in advance of the BRIGADE position who taken up during all day under heavy fire. Enemy eventually forcing these troops to withdraw. They broke however to HARDECOURT. 8th Rifle Brigade was 6 of high HAUT ALLAINES or to HARDECOURT, 8th Rifle next month no towards another 0 and B 2 & 8 K.R.R. next through to our position with its counter-attack being stopped they fell back to our position which was pushed through UPPER COURT of CLERY, where the remainder received through the night to road & received under Maj. C.C. Benjier's control Battn which for the night a T or R 10 L.B.R.	
	25th		Proceeded to TRONES WOOD - MARICOURT to relieve a Battn R 102nd RAR whilst waiting further order Command moved to and held GRAY - MEAULTE ROAD.	

WAR DIARY or INTELLIGENCE SUMMARY

Army Form C. 2118.

Place	Date	Hour	Summary of Events and Information	Remarks and references to Appendices
	March 5		In position N.E. of BRAY almost in due N. of BAPAUME at night, 1st/5th Bn. & Cav. to 62nd Bde Sch on 5th. About noon after heavy but chiefly hy. Shrapnel barrage we had to withdraw & position taken up in the La Boisselle West of BRAY, while the BRAY-CORBIE ROAD. The material of the line was a good deal of active enemy aircraft. Attempts not very much to collect stragglers from the units & others were then released to help in holding up the enemy, about 6.30pm who went up again. Coming to withdrawal of left flank men were ordered to withdraw as NCO to MORLAN COURT. During withdrawal message came through that we showing here in MORLAN COURT & we had to withdraw with all speed keeping south of the BRAY-CORBIE ROAD. Other four men assigned to form a screen out along the MORLAN COURT – BAILLY-LAFAYETTE ROAD and on the left being on the function to MORLAN COURT – BRAY-VAULX – SR 212 RS to cover the withdrawal of British troops. When all remained about an hour most of the time under rail & shell obtaining some strip into during this time a section of Cavalry outflanked our advanced intelligence machine gun. About 1pm all our troops being through we started intoxicating in Cavalry & KSC & KOYLI HQ 106 21 (6D) under Loss. Machine gun.	

WAR DIARY
or
INTELLIGENCE SUMMARY.

(Erase heading not required.)

Army Form C. 2118.

Place	Date	Hour	Summary of Events and Information	Remarks and references to Appendices
	March 26		In the direction of MERICOURT-L'ABBÉ enemy troops seen when the aeroplane returned to aerodrome. Pilot slightly wounded in foot.	
	27		SUERIE. At 5 a.m. 62nd Bgde Batn. took up position to support buthorpe Batn. next to RIBEMONT. No R.Eng Bgde supporting. Counter-attack. Huns were repulsed all along our front. Came through.	
	28		Enemy positions. Several counter attacks through shelling during the day which came through but in small parties with strong HEILLY support. The Non R.Eng Bde (300 Bn) moved back into position at all. Became the part until they 2 b. Battn.	
	29		Relief 10 p.m. relieved by 32 Australian Division. Unit arrived from 32 Australian Division. At HEILLY Reorganizing. Drew 3 boats ABC extc. Ancomont. Drew strength (officers 40 + OR)	
	30		At HEILLY 9.30 p.m. relieved by 105th Bgde and were held to move by buses to the line.	
	31		At MERICOURT, 1.30 p.m. marched to ALLONVILLE. arriving 4 a.m. Casualties in the fighting between March 21st — March 31st	

With Casualties marked (Missing, Wounded, Killed)
Officers	5	2
O.R.	26	134
		= 18 = 445 O.R.

C.O. 2/4th S.E. Rocdett RGA
C.M.E. Leicestershire Regiment

110th Brigade

atted. 21st Division

1/6th BATTALION

LEICESTERSHIRE REGIMENT

APRIL 1918.

WAR DIARY
or
INTELLIGENCE SUMMARY.

(Erase heading not required.)   6th Bn. Leicestershire Regt.

Army Form C. 2118.

Place	Date	Hour	Summary of Events and Information	Remarks and references to Appendices
	1918			
ALLONVILLE	1st April	5.0 A.M.	During the night 1st/2nd April the Bn. entrained at ST ROCHE AMIENS. Train left at 6 A.M. for 2nd Army Area. On arrival at destination HOPOUTRE S of POPRINGHE the Div came under orders of G.O.C. 1st Australian Div. The Bn proceeded from the station of detrainment by Motor Lorries to WAKEFIELD CAMP. LOCRE arriving at dusk April 2nd 18.	
LOCRE	Ap 2nd		Bn at WAKEFIELD CAMP. Draft of 1 Officer + 179 O.Ranks arrive	
			Gen Sir Herbert PLUMER G.O.C. 2nd Army inspected the Bn on arrival in the new AREA near LOCRE.	See Ap I.
		11 A.M.	The Bn moved to the WESTOUTRE AREA ALBERTA CAMP. M.5.a.4.12.	
WESTOUTRE AREA	Ap 3rd		Bn in ALBERTA CAMP.	

Army Form C. 2118.

WAR DIARY
or
INTELLIGENCE SUMMARY.
(Erase heading not required.)

Place	Date	Hour	Summary of Events and Information	Remarks and references to Appendices
WESTOUTRE AREA.	Ap 4th	3.30pm	Bn marched from Camp to RAMILLES CAMP KEMMEL. Draft of 283 O'Ranks arrive	Ap II
KEMMEL	Ap 5th		Training by Coys	
KEMMEL	Ap 6th		Training by Companies. Draft of Casuals arrive	
KEMMEL	Ap 7th		Bn Inspected by Maj Gen Campbell. G-O-C 21st Div	Ap III
		9.30pm	Bn moved to DE ZON Camp. Bn. H.Q established at M.12.c.8.3 Map Belgium 28	
	Ap 8th		Warning orders received that Brigade will move into WIELTJE AREA tomorrow.	
	Ap 9th		6th Bde relieve 5th B/o L Regt	
			Surplus Officers ~ O'Ranks ~ Transport march to MALPLAQUET ~ DICKEBOSH.	

WAR DIARY or INTELLIGENCE SUMMARY

Army Form C. 2118.

(Erase heading not required.) 6th Bn Leicestershire Regt

Place	Date	Hour	Summary of Events and Information	Remarks and references to Appendices
DE ZON CAMP.	April 9th	3.45 3.55	The Bn moved by two light Rly trains to LAMBTON, afterwards going into the line during the night 9th/10th/Ap.. The Div Sector being REUTEL-BEEK - TOWER HAMLETS 110th Bde. in the right Sub Sector, the 6th Bn Leic being on the left of the Bde. Sub Sector. 8th Bn Leic in Support. 7th Bn Leic in Reserve. Bn dispositions were:- A+B.Coy in Front line. C- Coy in Support + D in Reserve.	Ap IV
	10th		Patrols were sent out during night 9/10th but saw no sign of the enemy	
		11.45 AM	Rifle grenade shoot was carried out on the enemy front-line from our left front. C. Coy.	
		11.30	An enemy aeroplane taking advantage of the mist, flew low, about 50 feet + worked his machine gun on our trenches. Lewis gun + rifle fire was opened on him. Enemy Snipers were busy during the day, without any success. We established O.Ps. at J.20.0.70.15. at J.20.0.70.0.6. Our Snipers got 10 hours on several points + claimed one hit at J.21, 0, 3, 5.	

WAR DIARY or INTELLIGENCE SUMMARY

Army Form C. 2118.

6th Bn. Leicestershire Regt.

Place	Date	Hour	Summary of Events and Information	Remarks and references to Appendices
	April 11th		The Reserve Coy. "D" are now holding a line of steel tubes in DUMBARTON WOOD. Patrols out during the night 10/11th report no enemy seen. Listening post only manned owing to heavy rain in enemy trenches. The enemy attempted a raid on No 9 post of the Right Coy. but without success the N.C.O. of the 393 Regt was killed & identification obtained. Our Casualties nil.	
		11.45am	A party of 8 enemy wearing Goff Caps were seen in no mans land near JUTE COTTAGES making for our advanced Lewis gun post. They were fired upon, were seen to take the remainder attempted to run away or crawl back. Our Lewis gun opened fire wounding several. Casualties during day were: Officer Lieut C.R. FALLAS + 6 men wounded. 1 man gassed Total 8	65 RIR
	April 12th		Heavy rain throughout day. Reserve Coy. relieved D Coy. in the Right & C Coy. relieved B Coy in the Left. 1st War Companies by Lewis Night 12/13th were relieved by the 8 Leic during night 13/14th. Warning orders received that the Bn was to be relieved by the 8 Leic during night 13/14th. Right Coy during night 12/13 th erected wire in front of outpost. Left Coy employed in carrying up R.E. material. Support Coy improved PALESTINE WOOD trenches & made sniper posts. Parade day. day.	

Army Form C. 2118.

WAR DIARY
or
INTELLIGENCE SUMMARY.
(Erase heading not required.)

6th Bn Leicestershire Regt

Place	Date	Hour	Summary of Events and Information	Remarks and references to Appendices
	Oct 13th		Patrols out during night 12/13 Oct report 3 enemy seen in fortified shell hole at J.26.b.85.45.	
			Our Snipers engaged enemy snipers in their posts, one kill being claimed. A great deal of wiring has been done by the Right Coy during last 24 hours. The Left Coy erected wire in front of JULIA TRENCH. The Support Coy has improved STEVENS TRENCH & Cover in PALESTINE WOOD. Reserve Coy has been carrying up R.E. Stores from CANADA DUMP. Casualties during day. 1 O. Rank Killed.	App V
	Oct 14th		During night 13/14th the Bn was relieved by the 8th Leic the relief was completed by 9.30 p.m. On Completion of relief the Bn was accommodated in TUNNEL DUGOUTS. - CANADA STREET - HEDGE ST. - TORR TOP. with one section in each post in Corp line. The N.Z. Coy. taking part of Corp post line came under orders of the O.C. 6th Bn.	
		10. A.M.	Conference of Coy Commanders to discuss taking of Corp line.	
		10. P.M.	A & B. Coy reconnoitre Corp Res line Posts. Bde Commander held Conference of C.Os. at TORR. TOP. PRES. SALIENT. is being given up to enable a Corp to be drawn out into Army Reserve & to shorten line. The Bn less one Coy is to move back at dawn to ZILLEBEKE LAKE & work on a new line from FRENCH FARM. to CONVENT LANE. The N.Z Coy to move back at the	

WAR DIARY
or
INTELLIGENCE SUMMARY.

6th (R) Leicestershire Regt

Place	Date	Hour	Summary of Events and Information	Remarks and references to Appendices
	April 15th	7 AM	A withdrawal was made from YPRES SALIENT. The general line taken up was, for the Div. SNIPERS FARM inclusive O.1.c.3.4. to 1.21.c.6.0. jnd. N.E. of FRENCH FARM. The 7th Leic withdrew & went into reserve in HOWE CAMP & 8th Leic in support, occupying the G.H.Q. line between SHRAPNEL CORNER + BELLEGOED FARM. At this time the 110th Bde was holding the left Sub Section. One Coy of the 6th & later another Coy was sent up. The whole Commanded by MAJOR BURDETT. remained in front line of Corps front & acted a rearguard covering the withdrawal of the 7th & 8th Bn. from TOWER HAMLETS. These two Coys stood to at 4.45am & were ordered to remain in position until either the hour of withdrawal, or ordered to the embrasure, or completes to withdraw by the Enemy. On approaching their line, the rearguard Coys received orders to proceed by routes will stated route to BEDFORD HOUSE to report to Bn. A Small Party of selected men from the 7th & 8th Leic were left behind to hinder the Enemy's advance as much as they could by rifle fire & then to join C-Coy 6th Bn. The 6 Bn. H.Q. was established at BEDFORD HOUSE. " 7 " " " " HOWE CAMP " 8 " " " " FORRESTER CAMP " Bde H.Q. " " " " WALKER CAMP. 200 iron rations to be used on emergency ration were stored at BEDFORD HOUSE. Casualties during day 2 O. Ranks killed	

Army Form C. 2118.

WAR DIARY
or
INTELLIGENCE SUMMARY.
(Erase heading not required.)

6th Bn Berkshire Regt

Place	Date	Hour	Summary of Events and Information	Remarks and references to Appendices
	Ap.16th		Strong points established at BEDFORD HOUSE. 1 RoN BR.DE. 1 OLD FRENCH 1.3.b.7.8. Nucleus party move to MONTREAL CAMP. Casualties during day were 1 Officer LT A.M.LEE & 10.ORanks Killed, 4.O.Ranks Wounded Total 6	
	Ap.17th		The following relief took place during the night 16/17th Ap. 7th & 8th Leic. relieved two Coys of the 6th in the line CONVENT LANE to just N.W. of FRENCH FARM & the 6th Bn went into reserve on the line H.2.u.c.8.1. to H.3.a.c.3.3. HOWE CAMP being occupied for accommodation purpose. H.Q of the Bn was now at WHITE HOUSE. H.2u.C.1.1. Casualties during day were .O.Ranks 1 Killed 1 Wounded 2 missing Total 4	
	Ap.18th	5pm.	Orders were received to prepare all unnecessary bridges for demolition, to be destroyed under orders of Bn Cmdre. Bn H.Q. & A&B.Coy under Lieut.Col. E.S.CHANCE marched from HOWE CAMP. to TARR To b. to relieve MAJOR BORDETT. C&D Coys in Coyt line of posts. on Completion of relief MAJOR BORDETT'S PARTY. returned to G.H.Q Support line at HOWE CAMP.	Ap. VI

WAR DIARY
INTELLIGENCE SUMMARY
6th R. Inniskilling Regt

Army Form C. 2118.

Place	Date	Hour	Summary of Events and Information	Remarks and references to Appendices
	Oct 19th		Snow during the day. Good observation from O.Ps. at TORR TOP our artillery engaged many targets during the day	
	Oct 20th/21st	11.pm	Two Coys (C+D) of the Bn went to TARR TOP - HEDGE STREET, CANADA ST. TUNNELS. in support of the two Coys in Coy line of posts. MAJOR BURDETT from nucleus posts, also having one the two Coys. Lieut. Col. CHANCE is in command of Coys in line of posts	
		9.pm	S.O.S. was received by phone from Right Coy. post. CAPT. SCOTT. was sent out with party to clear up the situation.	
		10.30.pm	A message from CAPT. SCOTT saying post all right, send stretcher Bearers. The Right post held by LIEUT. VERNALL'S platoon had been raided about 9 pm. by a strong enemy party who crept up by OLD TRENCH to vicinity of post, also had an hour hand fighting the enemy were repulsed with considerable casualties to themselves. Rifles & equipment which had been discarded by the enemy were found near our post. Our casualties were slight about eight in number. Casualties during day were O'Rourke 3 Killed 14 Wounded 1 missing Total 18	

Operation Orders by Lt. Col. E.S. CHANCE Appendix VIII
22-4-18   Copy No 9

1. The Bn. will be relieved in the Corps Rest Line by OAK to-night April 22/23rd. Take over G.H.Q. Line from OAK on relief.

2. Advanced parties of OAK will be at I.24.d.3.3 Bulpots DRIVE at M.L.K-day. O.C. Coys PALM will arrange for guides to meet them there.
   Advanced parties of PALM will report to CAPT SCALES at 2p.m. to-day at I.24.d.3.3

3. 'A' Coy OAK will relieve A Coy PALM in Corps Rests.
   B   "   C   "
   C   "   B   "
   D   "   D   "

   A Coy PALM   A Coy OAK in G.H.Q Line
   B   B
   C   D
   D   C

   On relief PALM will be disposed as follows:-
   B.H.Q. — H.30.b.19
   A Coy in Right Reserve Line — H.Q. at H.30.b.1.4.
   B "   " Left   "   — HQ at H.30.b.1.4
   C "   Left Front Line — HQ LANKHOF FARM.
   D "   Right   "   — HQ IRON BRIDGE
                                  (I.26.c.2.6)

   Guides from advanced parties PALM will meet Coys. on relief as follows:-
   A Coy at BEDFORD HOUSE
   B "

WAR DIARY
or
INTELLIGENCE SUMMARY.

6th Bn Leicestershire Regt

Place	Date	Hour	Summary of Events and Information	Remarks and references to Appendices
	Ap 21st		Recapture of IMAGE WOOD continued in Bde orders for tomorrow. Redistribution of Coys during the night 21/22nd The Coys in front line, each with a platoon in outpost A.C.B. from the right. D in reserve. H.Q. 2 platoons at TORR TOP. 2 platoons in S.P. 94.1, ¼ mile W of TORR TOP. Casualties during day were O.Ranks 3 wounded 1 Gassed Total 4	Ap. VII
	Ap 22nd		During last night 21/22nd The following relief took place C Coy relieved A Coy in posts 1.30/1 + 1.30/2 on completion of relief B Coy relieved two Lewis Gun sections of A Coy who then reported to O.C.A Coy at CANADA STREET. Casualties during day were O.Ranks 1 wounded	

WAR DIARY or INTELLIGENCE SUMMARY

Army Form C. 2118.

6th Bn Leicestershire Regt

Place	Date	Hour	Summary of Events and Information	Remarks and references to Appendices
	Ap 21st		Recapture of MAGPIE WOOD contemplated. B.de asks for proposals. Redistribution of Coy's during the night 21/22nd. The Coys in front line, Back with a platoon in support. A.C.B. from the right. D in Reserve. H.Q. 2 platoons at TORR TOP. 2 platoons in S.P. 34. 1, 1/4 mile W of TORR TOP. Casualties during day were O.Ranks 3 wounded 1 gassed. Total 4	Ap. VII
	Ap 22nd		During last night 21/22nd. The following relief took place C Coy relieved A. Coy in posts 1.30; & 1.30/2 on completion of relief B. Coy relieved two Lewis Gun. Sections of A. Coy who then reported to O.C. A. Coy at CANADA STREET. Casualties during day were O.Ranks 1 wounded	

Appendix VIII

Operation Orders by Lt. Col. E.S. CHANCE Cmdg PALM
22-4-18
Copy No 9

1. The Bn. will be relieved in the Corps Rest Line by OAK to-night April 22/23rd & take over G.H.Q. line from OAK on relief.

2. Advanced parties of OAK will be at I.24.d.33 PUMPERS DRIVE at 4pm to-day. O.C. Coys PALM will arrange for guides to meet them there.
   Advanced parties of PALM will report to CAPT SCALES at 2pm to-day at I.24.d.33

3. 'A' Coy OAK will relieve 'A' Coy PALM in Corps Rest.
   B   C
   C   B
   D   D

   'A' Coy PALM   A Coy OAK in G.H.Q. Line
   B   B
   C   D
   D   C

   On relief PALM will be disposed as follows:-
   B.H.Q. — H.30.b.1.9
   A Coy in Right Reserve Line — HQ at H.30.b.1.4
   B   "   Left   "   — HQ at H.30.b.1.4
   C   "   Left Front Line   — HQ LANKHOF FARM
   D   "   Right   "   "   — HQ IRON BRIDGE
                                  (I.26.c.2.6)
   Guides from advanced parties PALM will meet Coys. on relief as follows:-
       A Coy at BEDFORD HOUSE
       B

Army Form C. 2118.

WAR DIARY
or
INTELLIGENCE SUMMARY.
(Erase heading not required.) 8th Bn. Leicestershire Regt.

Instructions regarding War Diaries and Intelligence Summaries are contained in F.S. Regs., Part II. and the Staff Manual respectively. Title pages will be prepared in manuscript.

Place	Date	Hour	Summary of Events and Information	Remarks and references to Appendices
	Apr 23rd		During the night 22/23rd the Bn was relieved in the Corps R of by the 7th Bn & took over the G.H.Q. line from the 7th on relief. Relief were as follows:- A. Coy 7th relieved A. Coy 6th Bn. : A. Coy 6th relieved A. Coy 7th Bn. B. " " " " B. " " : B. " " " " " B. " " C. " " " " C. " " : C. " " " " " C. " " D. " " " " D. " " : D. " " " " " D. " " On completion of relief the Bn's disposition were as follows:- Bn. H.Q. at H.30.b.1.9. A. Coy. Right Reserve line. H.Q. H.30.b.1.4. B. Coy Left Reserve line H.Q. h.30.b.1.4. C. Coy Left Front line LANKHOF FARM. D Coy. Right Front line IRON BRIDGE Casualties during day were O.Ranks 3 wounded	App VIII.
	Apr 24th		Fairly quiet day. Arrangements made & order to Corporals Bn about relieving our post day attacks & Trench Gd did tonight. During night a wire was received saying Germans would attack at 5 A.M. The relief of the reserve Coys was without incident and at D Coy received G.H.Q. line from Cheshire Regmnt. Casualties during day were O.Ranks 3 wounded 1 gassed Total 4	

WAR DIARY or INTELLIGENCE SUMMARY.

6th Bn Leicestershire Regt.

Army Form C. 2118.

Place	Date	Hour	Summary of Events and Information	Remarks and references to Appendices
	Apr 75	2.30 AM	Heavy hostile bombardment commenced. Batteries near Bn. H.Q. & Bn. H.Q. itself were bombarded with H.E. & gas shells till 5. AM. The area then became comparatively quiet. Gunners were led close to Bn H.Q. & were attended to by our M.O., one officer entered H.Q. runners dug out, all runners & signallers inside were gassed. The latter appeared to be near WYTSCHAETE our front was not attacked.	
		10. AM	Bn H.Q. heavily shelled, direct hit on kitchen. Mess. Transferred Bn H.Q. to SYAN CHATEAU ½ mile away where the 8th Leic were	
		11.45 AM	Flying patrol to standing post on the BLUFF returned, reported nothing in order on that front.	
		5.40 PM	Orders were received that the two Corps that had been holding the Day ordered during the vicinity of RIDGEWOOD (Bn. would be withdrawn & return to the 6th Bn Command at 9 p.m. under orders of O.C. No. 3 Pln.	
			The following readjustment of the line took place during night 24/25th. C/o 4 Pln of the 39th Co. R.E. Coy took over the defence of No. 8 Lock & VIMY Strong point. from D Coy. After handing over D Coy were accommodated in dugouts along the CANAL N of IRON BRIDGE & worked on the G.H.Q. line under the R.E.	App IX
			Casualties during day were ORanks 13 wounded & gassed. Total 17.	

Army Form C. 2118.

WAR DIARY
or
INTELLIGENCE SUMMARY.
(Erase heading not required.)   6th Bn Leicestershire Regt.

Place	Date	Hour	Summary of Events and Information	Remarks and references to Appendices
	Ap 26th		The enemy finally succeeded in taking St Eloi? On our troops from the ridge between HOLLEBEKE & WYTSCHAETE & there were no troops on the R of A Coy in G.H.Q.1 line O.C. 6 Bn sent up D Coy to fire up the gap on the right. The Composite Bde still held VOORMEZEELE. The Coy outpost line is to be withdrawn tonight. 7th Bn then became Bde Reserve. Casualties during day were O.Ranks 6 Killed 12 Wounded 8 Missing 3 Gassed Total 29	
	Ap 27th		D Coy was relieved in G.H.Q.1 line by a Coy of No 3 Composite Bn & occupies G.H.Q.2 line near CHATEAU SEGARD.	
		9pm.	About this time a man of C. Coy arrived at Bn H.Q. with information that C. Coy Hunter of LANKHOEF FARM had been captured by the enemy, this was confirmed from other sources. The 8th Bn sent one platoon towards LANKHOEF Fm. It was fired upon by machine guns. D Coy of the 7th Bn in G.H.Q.2 line was ordered to proceed up the CANAL & clear up the situation. About 3 A.M. 27/28 heard from O.C. of this Coy that Lock 8 was held by Composite Bde. Casualties during day were 1 officer 2Lt A.C. WATSON killed O.Ranks 1 Killed 16 Wounded 3 Gassed Total 21	

Army Form C. 2118.

WAR DIARY
or
INTELLIGENCE SUMMARY.
(Erase heading not required.)

Instructions regarding War Diaries and Intelligence Summaries are contained in F. S. Regs., Part II. and the Staff Manual respectively. Title pages will be prepared in manuscript.

Place	Date	Hour	Summary of Events and Information	Remarks and references to Appendices
	Ap 28th	4. A.M.	"D" Coy proceeded towards HAZELBURY FARM to clean up the situation. "C" Coy "post" were found to be strongly held by the enemy. Under the circumstances a counter attack with one Coy would have very little chance of success. During the reconnaissance of the front 2/Lt. EDEY + 2 men were wounded.	
			During the afternoon LOCK 8 was evacuated by the Bde on the right	
			The following relief took place during daylight today	
			Capt. VANNER'S Coy 7th Bn Leic. relieves our "A" Coy in G.H.Q.2 Line. Capt SCALES + 2 took up a position in G.H.Q.2 Line	Ap X
			"D" Coy forms a defensive flank from the R of the 8th Bn Leic Regt at HAZELBURY FARM to IRON BRIDGE inclusive	
			One platoon "B" Coy reported to O.C.B. + assisted to hold IRON BRIDGE Strong Point in relief of MAJ. TYLER's Coy of the 7th Bn	
			Casualties during the day were Officers 1 wounded 2 missing Ranks 4 killed 28 wounded 55 missing	
				Total 93.
			2/Lieut. EDEY belonged to 8th Bn Leic Regt	

WAR DIARY
or
INTELLIGENCE SUMMARY.

(Erase heading not required.) 6th Bn Leicestershire Regt.

Army Form C. 2118.

Place	Date	Hour	Summary of Events and Information	Remarks and references to Appendices
	Ap 29th	4 A.M.	Heavy Bomb.d opened, Gas shelling on Bn. H.Q., all lines down from Bde to Bn H.Q. Coys A. Coy & Bn relieved own own in G.H.Q line.	
		10.10 AM	O.C. D wires that right Coy given way & gave back beyond VOORMEZEELE	
		10. AM	D.C.A wires that his hdqrs were untenable & that he was retreating R + L	
		10.45am	B. Coy in G.H.Q line were heavily shelled throughout the day & had severe losses many men being buried	
		2.30pm	Enemy attacked D Coy who were holding IRON BRIDGE strong point, the enemy howls up the canal & his to support D Coy R. Flank. When the situation became known at Bn H.Q. Only 1 M. Gun Fire (both direct + indirect) from [was opened] on to the canal between IRON BRIDGE + LOCK 8 + on to VOORMEZEELE. This materially assisted D. Coy in repelling the attack & the enemy were driven back with severe casualties by Lewis Gun & Rifle Fire. At 10 o'R th enemy attacks on R. Platoon near KRUISSES STRAAT HOER - VOORMEZEELE ROAD had been driven off with loss. our losses 3 killed Hostile Arty very active from 9am to 3pm. Gas + H E shells being used. Gas shell hits on Bn H.Q. with 77 mm shells	
		10pm	50 R.E. & 100 pioneers arrived to dig switch trench posts between IRON BRIDGE + BELLEGOED FARM. These posts were dug & occupied by 1st Coy R.F. & 2 platoon Our Arty engaged targets on ridge during the day causing casualties to the enemy near LOCK 8 Casualties during the day were O. Ranks killed 6 Wounded 19. Missing 1 Total 20	
	Ap 30th		Quiet day. Bn to be relieved tonight by 9th R.W.F. + 6 WILT. REGT. 10 casualties during day were O Ranks 3 wounded	

Army Form C. 2118.

WAR DIARY
or
INTELLIGENCE SUMMARY.
(Erase heading not required.)

Place	Date	Hour	Summary of Events and Information	Remarks and references to Appendices

The undermentioned officers joined the Bn on date shown

2/Lieut W.R. Mieur 29-4-18   2/Lieut T.J Hodgkinson 1st-5-18   2/Lieut Mammatt 2-5-18
" Pegg 29-4-18   " M.Q. Purcell 1-5-18   " J Tapeix 2-5-18
" G.AU Squires 29-4-18   " Wilcox 1-5-18

Lieut G. Stevens 2-5-18   2/Lieuts Stauber 25-4-18
" J Osborne 2-5-18   " Clark 25-4-18
" J.S.M. Berneys 7-5-18   " Cooper 25-4-18
" Jeffries 25-4-18

Strength of Battalion 32 Offices 879 O/Ranks

Honours & Awards were awarded as under.

Major J.L. Burdett. M.C.   Legion D'Honneur (Chevalier)   Lieut J.H. Harratt } Military Cross.
                                                          " J.L. Rolash } 7-4-16.
Bar to Military Medal
10 3. 9   Corpl Botham T.

Military Medal

4440 21   Pte Dennis T.   9903 Pte Jurore P.J.   201924. Pte Cupin T.
16802.   Sgt Bloodworth. A. 16771 " MacR. T.   16265 Corpl Fowler J.M.
11496   Corpl Platts W.   11061 Corpl King W.   13246 Pte Foster H
40359   Pte Steele J.   33113 Pte Huxton W.   13612 Pte Hudson H.

Appendix II

Appendix III

SECRET.   Copy No. 9

Operation Orders No. 10 by   Lt. Col. E. J. CLARKE.
                                Commdg. 6th Bn. Leic. Regt.
B.E.F.   6.V.16.

1.   The Battn. will move from the SEAVAN Area to the
DE ZON Area to-day 7th inst.
        This Camp on being vacated will be occupied by
63nd Inf. Bde.
        Parade on "B" and "D" Coy's. parade ground at
2.20 p.m.
        MARCH OFF 2.30 p.m.
        ORDER OF MARCH. Hd. Qrs, "C", "D", "A", "B" and Transport.
        100 yards distance between Coy's. and Transport.
        On arrival in new area the Battn. will be billeted in
DE ZON Camp M.15.c.3.1. and BERMUDA Camp M.15.d.4.3.
        1 N.C.O. and 2 men per Coy. will report to Capt. SCALES
at Orderly Room at 10.30 a.m. to proceed as billeting party.
        Coy. Commanders will ensure that the present Camp
is left clean.

2.   BAGGAGE, ETC.   Officers' kits with valises and men's
blankets (tied in bundles of 10 and labelled) will be
delivered at Q.M. Stores by 11.30 a.m.

                                                    Lt.
                                A/Adjt. 6th Bn. Leic. Regt.

        DISTRIBUTION.
Copy No. 1. "A" Coy.   Copy No. 7 M.G.
        2.   "B"   "   8 Hd. Qrs.
        3.   "C"   "   9 War Diary.
        4.   "D"   "   10 Adjt.
        5.   M.O.   11 R.S.M.
        6.   T.O.   12 File.

Appendix IV

S E C R E T.   Copy No. 10

Operation Orders No. 1 By   Lt.Col. R. B. Clark.
                                    Comdg. 5th Bn.R.etc.Regt.
N.C.S.

Ref: MAP 1 : 1/40,000.

1. The Battn. will entrain at ARMENTIERES at 3.45 p.m.
to-day, detrain at LA BREE (I.2L.c.10.3.) and move into
the line to-night.
   Parade in camp ground by the Huts at 3.0 p.m.
   March Off 3.5.
   Dress: Assault Order; leather jerkins.
(Men not in possession of leather jerkins will wear great
coats).
   Rations for 10th inst. will be carried on the man.
   Lewis Guns and drums also two drums per Coy. will be
carried by the men.

2. ADVANCE PARTY.   Nucleus Party will parade in ....
at .... H.Q. & C.T. under 2/Lt. B. Paul.
   Parade 2.0 p.m.
   March off 2.10 p.m.
   Dress Marching Order.

3. TRANSPORT.   Transport Offr. will arrange to move the
transport in accordance with Administrative Instructions
No. 1.

                                    [signature]
                                    A/Adjt. for Lt.Col.
                                    Comdg. 5th Bn.Leicestershire Regt.

   DISTRIBUTION.

Copy No. 1. "A" Coy.   Copy No. 6. ....
      " 2. "B" "   "   7. H.Q. Offr.
      " 3. "C" "   "   8. Medical Off. Adv.
      " 4. "D" "   "   9. Any War Diary.
         5. ...   "   10. File.

Appendix IX

Operation Orders by Major O. B. Clark [...]

SECRET
                                                    Copy No 7

1.   On the following day of the BEDFORD
HOUSE [...] will take place to-night
        No 4 Pl. of the section to B. will take
over the defences at N.E. Corner & VIMY Strong Point
from D Coy of 6th [...] Regt.
        Relief will commence at 7:45 p.m.
        O.C. D Coy will report completion of relief
to Offr H Quigley Codes and GARNIER

2.   On completion of relief the remainder
of this Bn. will [...] LOCKE (incl) — IXII by
L. H. Co. A. [...] (incl) & H 20 central.

3.   One relieved D Coy will be accommodated in
[...] in the [...] N [...] Iron Bridge
[...] and the R.E.
        Latrines [...] with
[...]

4.   B. 3rd [inf] Bde take over the right half
of the 7th Can. Regt. in Corps Post leading to Mount
SORREL (incl) the right

5.   Acknowledge.

        DISTRIBUTION
        Copy No 1   O.C. A Coy
              2   B
              3   C   24
              4   D
              5 France   4/
              6 Nov[...]   18
              7 File

C Coy at LANKHOF FARM
　　　D "   IRON BRIDGE
　　　HQ "   WOODCOTE HOUSE

6. Guides of PALM Coys will meet OAK Coys
as follows:-
　　Guides   A & B Coys PALM at I 21 d 3.3. at 8.30 p.m.
　　　　　　C　　　　　　　　　　　　　 " 11.30 p.m.

D Coy PALM will not be required to send guides
to meet D Coy OAK.

7. Coy Cmdrs will ensure that all dugouts are
left clean.

8. Coy Cmdrs will ensure that each post is
handed over by an officer & that no garrison
is withdrawn until relieved.

9. On relief on the Reserve Coys will report to
Bn HQ by Cmdrs, and BANC (by runners)

10. On relief of OAK in OHQ Line, Coys
will report to Bn H.Q. by Cmdrs & BANC

11. All S.A.A., Sandbags, Trench Stores will
be carefully checked & handed over to OAK Coys.
A receipt will be obtained & forwarded to Bn H.Q.
as soon as possible after relief.

12. Receipts for stores taken over in GHQ
Line will also be forwarded to Bn H.Q. as
soon as possible.

13. Acknowledge

　　　　　　　　　　　G Pomeroy Lieut
　　　　　　　　　　　A/Adj PALM.

Appendix 1.

SECRET. Copy No. 9

Operation Orders No.11 by   Lt. Col. B. W. CHURCH,
                            Comdg. 6th N. Leic. Regt.
B.E.F.

1. The Battn. will move to the MELTOURNE area to-day 6th instant.
   Parade on road outside Camp at 10.55 a.m.
   March off 11.0 a.m.
   ORDER OF MARCH: H.Qrs., "B", "A", "D", "C" and Transport.
   100 yards distance between Coy's. and Transport.
   On arrival in new area the Battn. will be billeted in
   ALBERTA Camp H.Q. & A.B.

2. BAGGAGE ETC. Officers' valises and mens' blankets tied
   in bundles of 10 and labelled will be at the Q.M. Stores
   at 9.30 a.m.
   Coy. Commanders will ensure that all billets are
   left clean.

                                    B. Bruce
                                         Lt.
                    A/Adjt. 6th Bn. Leicestershire Regt.

DISTRIBUTION.

Copy No. 1. "A" Coy.   Copy No. 7 Q.A.
         2. "B" "   8 M. Gra.
         3. "C" "   9 War Diary.
         4. "D" "   10 Adjt.
         5. T.O.   11 R.S.M.
         6. M.O.   12 File.

SECRET   Appendix V No 7

1. 'A' Coy PALM will be relieved by 'C' Coy PINE
   'B'   "   "   "   "   " " 'D' "   "
   'C'   "   "   "   "   " " 'A' "   "
   'D'   "   "   "   "   " " 'B' "   "

2. ..... 'D', 'C', 'A'.
   And 'D' Coy PINE will ....
   Hrs. at 4.45 p.m.

3. O.C. 'D' Coy will arrange relief direct with O.C. 'B' Coy PINE.

4. S.P's 1, 2 & 3 of 'D' Coy will not be relieved till after dark.

5. All guides will be arranged between Coys concerned.

6. All maps, defence schemes, trench stores, will be handed over on receipt obtained. Receipts to be forwarded to Bn HQ as soon as possible after relief.

7. On relief the Bn will take over defence of the Copse Line. Orders as to dispositions will be forwarded later.

8. Excess from the cookers will be brought back. Dixies taken over from 5th Y + Lancs & all patrol kits will be handed over to PINE

...at... ...during the hours of
darkness.

(e) Coys will report relief complete to
Bn HQ. by codeword ABEL.
(f) Acknowledge.

Distribution
Copy No 1. OC A Coy Bn.
    2.   " B "
    3.   " D "
    4. Capt VANNER-OSC
    5. O.C. 17th Kings Liverpool Regt.
    6. File.

KB
for Rennes...
...
Kings ...

28.4.18

9. _munition_ _____ will be notified to
Bn HQ by code word "CAST"
10. Acknowledge

Distribution
Copy No 1. to A Coy
    2. " B
    3. " C
    4. " D
    5. " HQ
    6. " M.O
    7. " file
    8. " PINE
    9. " OAK
    10. " LEFT BN.
    11. T.O. &QM
    12. PRINCE

Division ___ sent
_____ to Lt Col.
Craig PALM.

12-4-18

Operation Orders by Lieut. Col. E.S.CHANCE Cmdg. PALM.
21-4-1918   Copy No.
                                             Appendix VII.

1. The following reliefs will take place to-night April 21st/22nd.

2. 'C' Coy will relieve 'A' Coy in posts I 30/1 A (the garrison will be increased to one platoon) & 'B' Coy in posts I 30/1 & I 30/2.

3. Reliefs will leave HEDGE STREET at 9.30 pm, where guides from 'A' Coy & 'B' Coy will report to O.C. 'C' Coy.

4. On relief 'B' Coy will relieve the two Lewis Gun Sections of 'A' Coy, which will report to O.C. 'A' Coy at CANADA STREET.

   Details of relief will be arranged between Coys. concerned.

5. All S.A.A, grenades, Very pistols & other trench stores will be taken over by 'C' Coy in the posts relieved & a copy of the receipts forwarded to Bn. H.Q.

   Completion of relief will be reported to Bn. H.Q. by runner by code word "HOOGE".

   Disposition reports will be forwarded by Coys. to Bn. H.Q. as soon after relief is complete as possible.

Distribution:-
Copy No.1 O.C 'A' Coy   No.4 O.C 'D' Coy
  "   2 " B   " 5 File.
  "   3 " C
                                    Adjt. PALM.

Operation Orders by OC F.S. CHANGE (illegible)

SECRET   Appendix X

1. The following dispositions will take place today:
   (a) Capt VANNERS Coy OAK will relieve A Coy PALM as soon as possible (during daylight) in G.H.Q. 1 line. A Coy PALM will in turn relieve Coy of 17th KINGS LIVERPOOL REGT (HQ H30 c.5.5), holding LOCK 8 (incl) up to CONVENT LANE (exclusive). A Coy will also occupy VIMY STRONG POINT with 1 platoon. OC A Coy will arrange details direct with OC 17th KINGS LIVERPOOL REGT.
   (b) D Coy PALM will form a defensive front from LOCK 8 (exclusive) to right of FINK at HAZELBURY FARM.
   Dispositions — 2 platoons along CANAL BANK between LOCK 8 & IRON BRIDGE. — 2 platoons between IRON BRIDGE & HAZELBURY FARM.
   One platoon of C Coy under 2/Lt JEFFERIES will report to OC D Coy at IRON BRIDGE STRONG POINT in relief of 1 platoon of Major TYLER's Coy OAK.
   (c) OAK is sending a Coy to occupy G.H.Q. 2 line in place of Capt VANNERS Coy.
   The Cmdr of this Coy will report to Capt VANNER at dug-out H.30. d.2.4. (Old Stores hold) but Capt VANNER will relieve A Coy PALM without waiting his arrival.
   (d) All Coys will take every precaution

SECRET   Appendix VI

To A & B Coys QM TD
Major Burdett   PRINCE

1. Bn HQ & A & B Coys will march at
5.0 p.m. to-day from HOWE CAMP to TORR
TOP to relieve Major Burdett & C & D Coys in
the Corps Line of Posts.

2. An advanced party of 1 NCO & 20 O.R.
per Bn HQ & A & B Coys will leave
HOWE CAMP at 2 p.m. to-day under Capt
SCALES. This party will report to Capt SCALES
at A Coy H.Q. at 1.45 p.m.

3. Major Burdett will send an advanced
party down to take over HOWE CAMP. This
party will leave TORR TOP about 6.30 p.m.

4. On relief Major BURDETT & C & D Coys will
march to HOWE CAMP.

5. Rations will be delivered at TORR TOP
this evening.

6. Major BURDETT & C & D Coys will relieve
Bn HQ A & B Coys in the Corps Line on
night 21/22nd

Culme Seymour   B Burdett
18.4.18   Lt Col

Army Form C. 2118.

WAR DIARY
~~INTELLIGENCE SUMMARY~~

The 6th Batt. Leicestershire Regiment

Place	Date	Hour	Summary of Events and Information	Remarks and references to Appendices
Batt. H.Q. SWAN CHATEAU.	MAY. 1st 1918		During the night 30th/1st May. the Bn. was relieved by the 9th R.W.F. + 6th Wilts. Regt. A.Coy. R.W.F. relieved B.Coy. 7th Bn Leic + platoons of that Bn on Right + Left of B.Coy 7th Bn. D.Coy. R.W.F. relieved B.Coy of this Bn + the platoon of B Coy 7th Bn that were oliveolis in the middle of B Coy of this Bn. C.Coy R.W.F. relieved two platoons of D under Lieut. ~~Baker~~ Chart: including advanced post at 1.25.b.3.0. with two sections. A new post has been dug at 1.25.b.2.4. + is now occupied by one platoon of C.Coy. R.W.F. Capt. Garnie's Force was relieved by D.Coy. R.W.F. A.Coy. of this Bn + 1 platoon of the 7th Bn that were in G.H.Q.2 line were relieved by by A.1.C. Coy 6th Wilts. at 9.p.m. April 30th. On completion of the relief the Coys marching by platoons moved via DEN GROENEN JAGER CABT. — WAD JUNCTION TO FARM. G.15.c.1.9.a distance of kilometres + rested until 2.30 p.m.	See Ap. I
		2.30 p.m	The Bn marched to the WATOU AREA + went into billets in the BOIS-DE-BEAUVOODE for the night 1st/2nd May, arriving there at 6.15 p.m. distance kilometres. Casualties O.Ranks 5 wounded	See Ap II

Army Form C. 2118.

WAR DIARY
INTELLIGENCE SUMMARY

(Erase heading not required.) The 6th Batt. Leicestershire Regiment.

Place	Date	Hour	Summary of Events and Information	Remarks and references to Appendices
Bois de BEAUVOORDE	May 2nd/18	9.10 a.m.	The Bn. marched to bivouac one Kilometre W. of BUYSSCHEURE in the LEDERZEELE AREA. A midday halt being made at a point 1 Kilometre W. of CASSEL and notwithstanding a long, tiring time in what was one hundred every member of the Bn. completed this march of approx 16 miles a wonderful to move off again 30 hours after.	See Ap III
BUYSSCHEURE	May 3rd		Remains in Bivouac	
BUYSSCHEURE	May 4th	5.20 a.m.	The Bn. marched to WIZERNES approx 15 K. where it entrained less one Coy (A). The train moved out at 11.30 a.m. & travelled via ST OMAR - CALAIS. - ABBEVILLE - ST DENNIS - FERE - EN - TARDINOIS to a siding near LHERY arriving the 4 p.m. The Bn then detrained & marched to camp 300 x E of LAGERY. a distance of approx 7 K. from the siding arriving in camp at 10 p.m. on the 5th. Entraining Strength :- 30 Officers 706 O Ranks Lieut Col Ct. Lawr Cmdg. Train	
LAGERY	May 5		En Route to LAGERY	
LAGERY	May 6th		A. Coy arrives in camp at 9.45 a.m. & the day was spent cleaning up in general	
LAGERY	May 7th		Coy Training commenced. Specialists under Specialist officers.	

Army Form C. 2118.

WAR DIARY
or
INTELLIGENCE SUMMARY.

(Erase heading not required.)

Instructions regarding War Diaries and Intelligence Summaries are contained in F.S. Regs., Part II. and the Staff Manual respectively. Title pages will be prepared in manuscript.

Place	Date	Hour	Summary of Events and Information	Remarks and references to Appendices
LAGERTY.	8th May		All Coys. Musketry on range 1 mile N of LAGERTY. during the day.	
LAGERTY	9 May		H.Q. Coy. + Lewis Guns on the range. A.B.C.D. Coys Training under Coy Commanders. Brigadier holds Tactical Exercise at 2 p.m. O.C. Coys + 2nd in Cmd of Coys attended. Capt. Scott. leaves the Bn. (S.R.) Capt G. Tooth joins the Bn. & took over the duties of Adjutant from Lieut. M.C. Poivance who becomes Intelligence Officer	
LAGERTY.	10th May		Training under Coy Commanders. A & B. Coys on the range during the morning	
LAGERTY.	11th May.		Training under Coy Commanders. O.C. & D.C. Coys visit line to be taken over by the Battn. Rouler. musk. Bombing Officer instructed in the use of French Bombs & Light Signals at Bde H.Q.	
-do-	12th		Reconnaissance of line held by 230" French Regiment carried out by Coys.	
-do-	13th		Bn marched from LAGERTY to CAMP de la TOUR near BOUVANCOURT arriving in CAMP at 2 p.m. Wt. stl. Chorus + 9 m. passed forwarded sick	

A5834 Wt. W4973/M687 750,000 8/16 D.D. & L. Ltd. Forms/C.2118/13.

Army Form C. 2118.

WAR DIARY
or
INTELLIGENCE SUMMARY.
(Erase heading not required.)

Instructions regarding War Diaries and Intelligence Summaries are contained in F. S. Regs., Part II. and the Staff Manual respectively. Title pages will be prepared in manuscript.

Place	Date	Hour	Summary of Events and Information	Remarks and references to Appendices
HERMINVILLE	May 14th		Bn left Camp de la Tour at 3 am and arrived in billets at Herminville at 9.15 am. Day spent making final arrangements for relieving one Bn in line held by the 6th Bn of 230th French Regiment.	
In the line sector de la Côte between Canroy- Cormicy	May 15th to May 20th		Sector extremely quiet. Only six shells burst during the whole of this period in the Bn Sector. Enemy patrols were active, twice entering our lines, first at the head of the Trinité boyaut - once the night of 16/17 and once on 18/19 - when we had evacuated it. On patrols were also active. There were no casualties through the war. Bn was relieved by the 20th Leicesters R. on the night of 20/21st.	
CAUROY LE VERGEUR	May 21st to 26th		Bn in Divisional Reserve at "D" Camp, CAUROY - Le - VERGEUR. First two days spent in cleaning up and reorganized on remainder to being devoted to training. The Brigadier found H.R. Cummings- instructed H.Q.Bn on the 23rd; Bn was taken to relieve the Public Leicestershire R in the left subsector of the front. Intended to be postponed owing to information being received that our missing attack would take place about on 27th.	

WAR DIARY or INTELLIGENCE SUMMARY.

Army Form C. 2118.

Place	Date	Hour	Summary of Events and Information	Remarks and references to Appendices
CHALONS-le-VERGEUR	May 27	1 am	Enemy commenced heavy bombardment with gas and H.E. on Stand. The Battalion left at 12.45 p.m. & endeavoured to dug outs and shelters in vicinity of Bn H.Q. as soon as bombardment commenced. A Coy under Capt Rolt M.C. had been moved up to the "Tranche de Buires" E of CORMICY on the night of May 26th and exposed in positions about 3 ft.	
		3 am	Few shells & cased but concentration of gas shell and other such shells	
		4 am	Tranche de Buires heavily bombarded until 5 am	
		7.30 am	B Coy (Capt Oakley) moved forward to Bde Hq. on Bois de la Miniere as a forward Reserve to Bn de ESTERNEY with right on OURVRAGE de N. NORD and left on NEUVE WOOD	
		9 am	D Coy and two M.g. moved forward to Red H.Q. A Coy heavily attacked in Tranche de Buires but held some Italian off by rifle and Lewis gun fire	
		11.30 am	C Coy (Lt Plowrey) moved forward and organised remainder of Bn in vicinity of 110th Bde H.Q. in Bois de MINITA CROIX	
		12 noon	Tranche de Guise again heavily attacked. Enemy soon repulsed & rights lost. Succeeded in establishing posts on the right and left flanks which eventually forced the remnants of the Coy under Corporal B— to withdraw to a Br de ESTERNEY in front of CAUROY - CORMICY R	
		2 pm	Bn H.Q. moved to the TUILERIE Bn was moved up to position near Bryan de Brice about right and left in front of CAUROY - CORMICY R, together two groups with R Coy on right but total could not be obtained. C Coy on left. Consequently there was a Gap of over 1000 yds on the left.	

A 5834 Wt. W4973/M687 750,000 8/16 D.D. & L. Ltd. Forms/C.2118/13.

Army Form C. 2118.

WAR DIARY
or
INTELLIGENCE SUMMARY
(Erase heading not required.)

Place	Date	Hour	Summary of Events and Information	Remarks and references to Appendices
	May 27"			
		2.30pm	C. Coy ordered forward to fill gap between A&D Coys, keeping 1 platoon in reserve at Bn. H.Q. Touch was obtained with Bn on right and 1 platoon detailed to form a defensive flank facing CORMICY. Repeated attempts have been made to establish touch with the troops holding CORMICY.	
		4pm	Enemy attacked up to the ESTERNAY from TROSSY to CAUROY. Attack was through the trenches & till on right and enfilading fire about 750 yds. from TO ESTERNAY	
		5pm	Under cover of dead ground the enemy succeeded in establishing a footing in ##### wood on the right flank of D Coy. He also threw repeated bombs in the direction of VPM hill & was repulsed each time with heavy losses.	
		7pm	Reinforced by T.M's. Enemy succeeded in breaking the line of the right flank of D Coy. Posts were immediately established in the houses on the trench width in enemy held up the attack.	
		7.30pm 8pm	Enemy threatening the left flank of C Coy from direction of CORMICY. Enemy hooking around the left rear of C Coy and firing into them from open ground & distillation on right flank of D Coy. Bty formed a defensive flank along the Bayard de CAMP 1220 M.	
		10pm	Enemy continued to work round flanks up to A & D Coys in considerable cover of darkness.	

2449 Wt. W14957/M90 750,000 1/16 J.B.C. & A. Forms/C.2118/12.

Army Form C. 2118.

WAR DIARY
or
INTELLIGENCE SUMMARY
(Erase heading not required.)

Instructions regarding War Diaries and Intelligence Summaries are contained in F.S. Regs., Part II, and the Staff Manual respectively. Title Pages will be prepared in manuscript.

Place	Date	Hour	Summary of Events and Information	Remarks and references to Appendices
	May 27	11pm	Orders received from Bde (B & 5th/7 attached) to withdraw to the line of BOUZINCOURT - ROUEZ RIDGE covered by rearguard. Withdrawal commenced up to line ordered & rearguards and covermts of 5/7 Bn 5/7 in BOUZINCOURT and & 6th Bns had considerable difficulty in recovering their cars and arranging to withdraw fighting a rearguard action.	
	May 28"	2.45 am	Bn arrived at the junction of the CHALONS - KAPPENBERG - HERMONVILLE - BOUZINCOURT Rd. Bn after a period of halt up a position along ridge running from BOUZINCOURT - HERMONVILLE Rd but consequently ordered to march to POTY-PROTECTS arriving at 3.45am.	
		4am	Bn marched to LUTHERNAY FARM on the POTY - HERMONVILLE Rd. Bn arrived there. Two Coys (C&D) were encountered by a hostile a/c and the 2 Coys in B AUBORNE. 2nd. Right flank was in touch with the other (?) from the 1st bn on the left.	
		6am	Enemy attacked LUTHERNAY FARM from direction of FRY - JARBORENT. No R & O Bn went up positions N & of the POTY - HERMONVILLE / PERRY - JARBORENT.	
		7am	Coy. attacks a Coy forced a defensive flank from BAUBOURG to the POTY - HERMONVILLE Rd. Attacked left flank of brigade.	
		7am - 3pm	Along the fight ensured which brought the enemy attack to a standstill roughly along the line of the POTY - HERMONVILLE Rd. N & of Chau MERILLON	

WAR DIARY
or
INTELLIGENCE SUMMARY

Army Form C. 2118.

Place	Date	Hour	Summary of Events and Information	Remarks and references to Appendices
		1pm	On both flanks the enemy seemed to be making progress. Troops were now seriously pressed with troops from 25 Division and French troops	
		2.30pm	French reported that they were withdrawing S.W. of Ch. NEUVILLON as they had been outflanked	
		3pm	After covering the withdrawal of French & Battalion fell back to new area by platoons but before this could be accomplished the enemy charged from the left flank. Heavy fighting took place in the line of the old German line at first resulting in holding up of the enemy by our officers & Lewis gun to allow the troops N. of L'ECLUSE Farm to withdraw. Positions were held up by this but nine were completely shot up. The French on the ridge N.W. of PRISNY Bois by this time were completely shot up by machine gun fire and men fought under the orders of individual officers.	
		5pm	It had become who had been wounded, collected somewhere and marched out to Beaulieu Rosoy. Remainder of officers, what were remained detached, reported to W.O. Sanger 1050 at TILLOY NEUF COURCELLES - SAPICOURT and to the R/o a line along the railway between	

WAR DIARY or INTELLIGENCE SUMMARY

Army Form C. 2118.

Place	Date	Hour	Summary of Events and Information	Remarks and references to Appendices
	May 29	9 am	Jerry shells fires opened from RESMAN and two M.G. fires from West of Hill 202. Artillery was put down to [?] the advance. Situation at BRANSCOURT and a few hundred yards to S.W. but front [?] of Battalion N. of Hill 202. The enemy attacked during the attempt, about 40 O.R.'s also [?] in this period of the attempt. Remainder were at all times in close [?] of being advanced over the BRANSCOURT valley. The General tendency of all enemy movement at the MARNE was opposite front L.A. h. along the BRANSCOURT-TRESLON Road was westerly [?] and guns were moved even like an axis at a [?] was too long to settle for Batteries. At the middle hill to woods TRESLON Trees were observed withdraw of E.A.E. of Infantry and [?] to [?] 26 Division reported attack on the N.W. of Hill of the 19th and E[?]. Battalion in [?] action on the W. of the 5/R. LUSMAN-TRESLON Rd. out troops in front of Hill 202 and a battalion of French Tirailleurs was attack [?] BRANSCOURT S. but that actually was placed in straight from Branscourt S. [?], [?] enemy attacked in rifle and M.G. fire and attack [?] to a standstill afterward [?]	

WAR DIARY
or
INTELLIGENCE SUMMARY
(Erase heading not required.)

Army Form C. 2118.

Place	Date	Hour	Summary of Events and Information	Remarks and references to Appendices
			Touch was obtained with B Coy (Capt Turner) and Coy was ordered to take up a position of readiness in ground near Rossway Farm. Some enemy still making progress of Hill 202, and several enemy near Trefcon Copse to Hill 202 all attempts to advance were held up by our rifle + M.G. fire.	
		7.45pm	Enemy commenced heavy bombardment of front on Hill 202 with Field Guns of horse Artillery and heavy minenwerfer. Their choice of our hurried tracing and skillful handling of troops had enabled Bn to maintain its position throughout day was then commenced withdrawing another line was occupied & run directly Hill 202 facing Trefcon C.S. There were over about 30 British troops left with the French. The French on right withdrew in conformity with this movement to COURCELLET—SAULCOURT. C/Sgt James with his Coy of 8th 6ORR placed at the disposal of Major Strudwick moved to support 24 Colonel moved Infantry and took up a position in front of Rossway Farm together with our Fallen Guns. This position was maintained until dawn when troops were relieved and Bn K withdrew Bn and concentrated in MERRY-NANCY which are de-billeted attach page 30f	

WAR DIARY
or
INTELLIGENCE SUMMARY

(Erase heading not required.)

Army Form C. 2118.

Instructions regarding War Diaries and Intelligence Summaries are contained in F.S. Regs., Part II. and the Staff Manual respectively. Title Pages will be prepared in manuscript.

Place	Date	Hour	Summary of Events and Information	Remarks and references to Appendices
	May 30th		Bn march to Bernas to FOUREY arriving about 8.30am to bivouac. Bn moved to bivouac in wood 2 miles west of Bernaucourt in evening	
	May 31st		Bombed & attacked by night. Casualties from May 1st to May 31st 1917. OFFICERS: Lt Col. E.S. Burns Killed in action. Lieut. A.W. Pickard wounded in action. 2/Lt C.B.E. Noel — ditto — 2/Lt W.R. Escourt — ditto — 2/Lt G. Legge — ditto — Capt. J. Legg M.C. missing 2/Lt W.E. Thurso — ditto — 2/Lt A.J. Clark — ditto — 2/Lt E.A. Austin — ditto — 2/Lt A.A. Bywater — ditto — 2/Lt A. Collis wounded in action. OTHER RANKS: Killed 32 Wounded 99 Gassed 1 Drowned 144 missing believed w. 3 Total 11 Officers 278 O.R.	

4.6.18.

J.C.Burdett Major
Commanding 2/5th Bn The Leicestershire Regt.

Army Form C. 2118.

WAR DIARY
or
INTELLIGENCE SUMMARY
(Erase heading not required.)

6th Bn Leic. Regt.

Place	Date	Hour	Summary of Events and Information	Remarks and references to Appendices
Lievin	June 1st 1918		A composite company was formed out of the Bn. under Lt Widdin & moved by lorry route along with two more companies from the 4th & 5th Lie the whole under Lt Col Irwin D.S.O. to take up position N.W. of the Marne & N.W. of Dormant. The remainder of the Batt:n remained in billets in Lievin until the morning of June 3rd	Ref Map Chalons Amiens 1/80,000
	3rd		Orders were received to move to new area at 6 A.M. & Bn. normally moved route to Courjonnet 6 miles S. of Espres, & there remained in billets until June 9th	"
	5th		Reinforcements of 2 Offs & 26 O.R. were sent to joined the Composite Coy which was still holding the position as afore. Party proceeded 1/45 hrs & proceeded by lorry route. Further small party of Sany Orders were received to move with 9 Offs & 6 a new area one days march South	"
	9th		Composite. Destination known. Bn marched of 10.30 P.M. arrived at Moury 5 A.M. halting for dinners at a point 600 Yds E of Chalon. Route M LEVENARD to Route 57 – Bouy – aux – Bois, Chalon. Vercy. Moury. billeted for the night.	"
	16th		Batt:n remained in billets at Moury until the morning of the 16th. During the intervening days: training was carried out; gas equip/ment completed as far as was possible.	"

35.2

WAR DIARY
or
INTELLIGENCE SUMMARY

(Erase heading not required.)

6th B" Leic Regt

Army Form C. 2118.

Place	Date	Hour	Summary of Events and Information	Remarks and references to Appendices
Moeuvres	June 14 1918		On the morning of June 14th orders were received for the 2/2nd Division less the 2nd Independent Brigade to move by Rail to the Offreville Area. The 6th B" Leic. Regt. moved in accordance with the orders proceeding by lorry route to entraining station Gommecourt via Sequine. Commencing Halt: Gommecourt, Sommecourt. Left Moeuvres 9 A.M. June 14th, arrived entraining station 11 A.M. Entrained 5.37 P.M. The Transport left Moeuvres at 12.30 along June 13th to entrain as arrangements billeted at Gommecourt for the night rejoining the B" at Gommecourt.	Re Map North West Europe Sheet 10 1/253,000
Hangest	June 15 " June 16		B" detrained at Hangest (Somme) & encamped for the night in the village. B" entrained at Hangest at 1.15 A.M. for destination Ramburies detrained 15 miles. Arrived Ramburies 12.30 & billeted in village until June 22nd. Training & re-equipping was continued with during the period of rest.	Re Map France Sheet 17 1/100,000
Rambures	June 19th		The Company in the 2/2nd Independent Brigade re-formed the B" from the on June 19th.	
"	June 22		Orders were received to move by March Route to le Mesnil Recurme distance 15 miles. Route B of Boultencourt - Aumation - Souvring - X Roads 1/2 mile S.E. of Vm L'Epinoy - Bargmont - Guerville - Milleville. March was carried out as a Brigade à Balle ready 1/4 rendezvous at Starting Point X Roads 1/2 mile W of Witlhem at 10 A.M. on June 22 nd	Re Map France Sheet 16 1/100,000

Army Form C. 2118.

WAR DIARY
or
INTELLIGENCE SUMMARY

(Erase heading not required.)

6th Bn. Leic. Regt.

Instructions regarding War Diaries and Intelligence Summaries are contained in F. S. Regs., Part II. and the Staff Manual respectively. Title Pages will be prepared in manuscript.

Place	Date	Hour	Summary of Events and Information	Remarks and references to Appendices
Bayenval	June 30/1918		Battn. Halted for dinner outside the village of Bayenval for 1½ hours, nearer destination 5 P.M. Battn. remained billeted in the village until July 1st when it moved by Rail to Puchevillers Area. During the war period training was carried out and re-equipment was almost completed.	Map Ref. Sheets 51b & 16 1/100,000
Sheet Reanno June 30			Transport of B.E. moved by Road to Puchevillers Area; halting for the night June 30/July 1st in Accamonst Area; & for the night July 1/2. Hangest. Total Casualties for period June 1st to June 30th 1918:- # Other Ranks. Wounded.	

8/7/18.

W. Morton
Lt. Col.
Comdg. 6th (Ser.) Bn. The Leicestershire Regt.

Army Form C. 2118.

WAR DIARY
or
INTELLIGENCE SUMMARY.
(Erase heading not required.)

5th B. Lincolnshire Regt.

Place	Date	Hour	Summary of Events and Information	Remarks and references to Appendices
Gherie Beaume	July 1st		Battalion moved by march route to Ervillers [?] for Divisional Reserve. Battn. moved off [?] and arrived at entraining station 9/am [?] bivouaced in field for the night & entrained 7 pm on arrival at July 2. Battn detrained @ Belencourt Station at 4 am & proceeded Anqueres by march route, & arrived [?] billets.	
	2nd		Programme of training was commenced	
Anqueres	3rd 4-7		Training continued on interior Economy Reals Lewis Gun & Rifle Ranges daily	
"	5th		2nd in Command Coy. Company Commanders reconnoitred Brown Line where fresh positions would be manned in the event of hostile attack, and Lachichen [?] marked. Training continued in Musketry, visual selection & one order Drill &c.	Stel/57 D S.E. 1/20,000
"	6th & 7th 8-13		One officer & one NCO per Coy. were daily reconnoitred these positions in Brown Line. Training on above continued.	
"	on the night of July 13th/14th Practice Stand-to was carried out with a view to seeing to how far Battn. was ready for battle as no less ready to move to area reported by Battalion within forty five minutes of alarm being given. Church Parade & Baths for Battalion.			

WAR DIARY
or
INTELLIGENCE SUMMARY.
(Erase heading not required.)

6th Batt. Leicestershire Regt.

Army Form C. 2118.

Place	Date	Hour	Summary of Events and Information	Remarks and references to Appendices
Argueves	July 14		C.O. 2nd in Command, Adjt & Coy Commanders proceeded by lorry route to Engelbelmer to reconnoitre section of Battle front held by 1/7 R.W. at present. Intention is to relieve 1/5th Brigade 38th Division with a view to relieving same on the night July 14/15th. Senior reconnoitred known "Leavard Section."	Ref map sheet 57 D S.E 1/20,000
	15th		Brigade Inspection by G.O.C. 5th Corps on ground near Head Quarters were presented to Officers 1/9 R. by Corps Commander as awards during operations [?] March 21st 1915 - May 3rd 1916.	"
	16th		Training during morning. Divisional Commander addressed all officers O.R. [?] were not addressed by him at Chalons the Battle March 21st O. who were not addressed by him at Chalons la Verge May 19th. Battalion moved by march route to relieve 5th [?] night July 16/17th in telephone com with a new trenches 1/7 R.W.[?] in the usual section until the following night.	
	17th	9 p.m.	Orders were received enabling relief, the Battn to proceed	
	"		Here to Forme Killvels in Argueves Battn moved by march route trace totally uneven, unexpected from Killvels	

Army Form C. 2118.

WAR DIARY
or
INTELLIGENCE SUMMARY
(Erase heading not required.)

Of Battn. Suspensive Ray

Place	Date	Hour	Summary of Events and Information	Remarks and references to Appendices
ACHEUX P.15.d.2.8.	July 1917 22nd	6.45 pm	Battalion paraded to move up the line. Relieved 4th Bn R.S. in Reserve Posn. 1901. Bgh Ride in BROWN SYSTEM at P.15. S.d., P.15.a.5., & P.30 pm. Relief took place without casualties during very quiet.	28 May SE. 1.25.N.W.
"	23rd			
"	24th	8.30 pm	Section, Platoon and company training carried out. Battalion in BROWN SYSTEM. Battalion moved by route march to relieve 11th Border at 3 nukh hours. Battalion relieved 11th Border from QUAKER ALLEY to DRAKE ALLEY. 2 coys in front line one in support. Battn. HQrs. at Q.22.d.3.c.	
"	25th		Our patrols encountered strong hostile posns E. of Welsh arg. q.23.d. at farm further dispersed. Two were probably killed. One casualty by enemy MGs shelled on afternoon with T.mor & 150 mm HE. & 8" & 2.10 & 2.2 am at intervals.	
"	26th	4 am 6 pm	Our strong patrols brought in two y of an N.C.O. of 14th (?) Infty Regt. 3 1st hand at Hermies. A second patrol left our lines at Q.23.a.4.16.20. 10.30 pm will object of surprising enemy MG Post at Q.23.a.6.7. It was attacked with rifle grenades and MGs. There was no casualties. There many grenadiers and MGs. The patrol withdrew at 4.30 am without casualties. Quiet at T.M. fire. Our afternoon and evening minenwerfers being highly active during day.	
"	27th		Our patrols were out during the hours of darkness to locate enemy front line. Enemy highly alert ... T.mors HE and MGs on the morning.	

Army Form C. 2118.

			Army Form C. 2118.

WAR DIARY
or
INTELLIGENCE SUMMARY.
(Erase heading not required.)

Place	Date	Hour	Summary of Events and Information	Remarks and references to Appendices
	July 28th	10 pm	Dispositions of Battn. readjusted. One coy in front line (intermediate dispositions in support to INTERMEDIATE ZONE and one coy in PURPLE LINE and one company of O.C. Support Battn. Battn HQs opened at Q.26.a.5.2. Radical mans of O.C. Support Battn. Battn. Back'n. drawn by near CHARLES AV. and to DRAKE ALLEY incl. Rugbo and Back'n.	Ref. Map Sht Jul 57 B S.E.1/20,000
	29th		Hostile artillery and machine guns active all day on mostly ENGLEBELMER and valley in Q.26.a. intermittently shelled with 105 with HE and Blue Cross gas. Our observing patrols our owing to hours of darkness within our own lines saw nothing of the enemy.	
	30th		Enemy attack near Oulive louis Brent'z companying smoke screen fronted at 04:00 hrs by our TMB front and was quickly resumed our fire support at once. Machine gun fire with light trench mortars our own fire type and screening smoke. Hundreds of 77mm and 105mm HE and Whiz Bang Tracks throwing S.E. from ENGLEBELMER TRENCH were continually shelled with 150mm HE.	
		9:00 pm	Became battn. in support again and relieved 7th Bn. the coloniale Regt. Bn. HQs established at Q.19.c.7.6.5. in PURPLE SYSTEM. One Company Battn. which was sent forward the suffering two casualties from shell fire whilst on O.B. to its supply & eating occupied and whose 10 yards from and other whilst our heavy bombarded with high explosive shells and MG. Part was already taken & the position had not any support.	
	31st		Interior economy. One company ordered with move R.E. supply in PURPLE SYSTEM.	

WAR DIARY.

PLACE	DATE	HOUR	Summary of Events and Information.	Remarks and References to Appendices
	25-7-18 to 31-7-18		CASUALTIES. 1. OFFICER. 2nd Lt. W. R. MILLER. Wounded in Action 4.25-7-18. 4. O.Rs. Killed in Action. 17. O.Rs Wounded in Action.	

M. Murphy
Lt. Col.
Comdg. 6th Bn Line Regt.

2/4/6

Confidential.

War Diary.

August 1918.

6th Bn Leicestershire Regt.

Army Form C. 2118.

WAR DIARY
or
INTELLIGENCE SUMMARY.
(Erase heading not required.)

Instructions regarding War Diaries and Intelligence Summaries are contained in F. S. Regs., Part II. and the Staff Manual respectively. Title pages will be prepared in manuscript.

Place	Date	Hour	Summary of Events and Information	Remarks and references to Appendices
ENGLEBELMER	Aug 1st to Aug 4th		Battalion in Brigade Reserve in PURPLE SYSTEM. Working parties found to improve trench system, construct dugouts etc. One company in Palluming for patrol's wire which found patrolling and reconnoitring patrols nightly sent out in vicinity of HAMEL.	
	Aug 5th	10 pm	Relieve the 2nd/4th York & Lancs Regt in the HAMEL Sector. Battalion front extending from ETON LANE to CHARLES AVENUE. Two coys in front line and in support, one in reserve at Br Commdr. H.Q.	
West of HAMEL	Aug 6th Aug 13th Aug 14th Aug 15th Aug 16th		Battalion dispositions unaltered. No same system. Snipers company lively carried out. Our night line was advanced to nearer ANCRE through old enemy lines above line held. Our night line patrols were established. Battalion holding line of river ANCRE from STATION ROAD (S.E. of BEAUMONT-HAMEL) to HAMEL inclusive. At night time line being held endeavoured to cross the ANCRE but failed.	
	Aug 17th		Battalion holding same line. On night patrol was winked by German Regt.	
ENGLEBELMER	Aug 18th	4 am	Battalion arrived in PURPLE SYSTEM in Brigade Reserve. Parties found to work in PURPLE SYSTEM and MAILLY - MAILLET.	
	Aug 19th Aug 20th		Working parties continued to be found as above. Battalion prepared to move up to assembly positions for attack on THIEPVAL RIDGE (N of THIEPVAL).	
N.E. of HAMEL	Aug 21st	4 am	Battalion in assembly positions on river ANCRE.	

WAR DIARY or INTELLIGENCE SUMMARY

Army Form C. 2118.

Place	Date	Hour	Summary of Events and Information	Remarks and references to Appendices
	Aug 21st		Two companies advanced across river at dawn and completed to withdraw owing to strong hostile opposition	
		4 pm	Both companies reoccupied west side of river, having been badly shaken. Later they were withdrawn to old front line.	
			Remaining two companies in reserve positions till night, when fighting patrols were sent out. These patrols advanced our ridge —	
	Aug 22nd	6 am	Whole Battn in two companies advanced over river and commenced running advance established themselves in first objective (enemy trenches) running NE along ridge about 80 yards from river.	
		8 pm	First objective attached. later Battalion relieved by 6th Bn Dorset Regt.	
ENGLEBELMER	Aug 23rd	5.30 am	Battalion identified in PURPLE SYSTEM.	
		5 pm	Marched via BEAUMONT-HAMEL and BEAUCOURT to LITTLE TRENCH (1000 yds S.W. of BEAUCOURT and E. of ANCRE)	
	Aug 24th		Attacked and took BATTERY VALLEY and BOOM RAVINE (S.W. and E. of GRANDCOURT respectively.) At night advanced to HH PYS.	
	Aug 25th		Followed through LE SARS to EAUCOURT L'ABBAYE	
		4 pm	Hostile counter attack repulsed in Madaloin at latter place, after which a dismount flank to Bucrenous was found facing South.	
	Aug 26th / Aug 27th		Moved to WARLENCOURT. (Brigade now in Divisional Reserve)	
			Assembled to attack LE BARQUE. Attack cancelled. Battalion returned to WARLENCOURT.	
	Aug 28th	9 pm	Left WARLENCOURT and relieved 2nd Battn Lincoln Regt East of the BUTTE DE WARLENCOURT	

Army Form C. 2118.

WAR DIARY
or
INTELLIGENCE SUMMARY.
(Erase heading not required.)

Instructions regarding War Diaries and Intelligence Summaries are contained in F.S. Regs., Part II. and the Staff Manual respectively. Title pages will be prepared in manuscript.

Place	Date	Hour	Summary of Events and Information	Remarks and references to Appendices
	Aug 29th		Battalion in Brigade Reserve. Tommy continued to withdraw. Battalion followed up to LUISENHOF FARM (S. 28 THILLOY) and bivouacked.	
	Aug 30th		Remained in above position.	
	Aug 31st	10 pm	Left LUISENHOF FARM to assume positions 500 yds West of RIENCOURT astride BAPAUME—PERONNE ROAD. Outposts on BRAUNCOURT from N.W. as follows: 2 AM following morning.	

Casualties during month of August 1918.

OFFICERS. Lt. Col. H.C. Martyn. D.S.O. M.C. Missing 26.8.18.
       Capt. J.R. Jardine   Killed   23.8.18.
       2/Lieut W.M. Gollogly   "   26.8.18 (D/w 23.8.18)
       Lieut M.H. Girvan, M.C. Wounded 31.8.18 (D/w 23.8.18)
       "   M.J. Rogers   "   22.8.18.
       "   G.E. Walther   "   23.8.18.
       "   T.J. Hodgkinson   "   9.8.18.
       Lieut. H.S. Wilde   "   15.8.18.

OTHER RANKS.   Killed (& died of wounds)   21
             Wounded   174
             Missing   6
             TOTAL   204

9.9.18

C. Burdett. Major.
Commdg. 6th (S.) Bn. R. Leicestershire Regt.

Army Form C. 2118.

WAR DIARY
or
INTELLIGENCE SUMMARY.
(Erase heading not required.)

Sept 1918   L.N.Lan Regt

Place	Date	Hour	Summary of Events and Information	Remarks and references to Appendices
BEAULENCOURT	1st	2.30 a.m.	Brigade attack on BEAULENCOURT. 6" Bn on left, 7/Lincolns in centre, 1600 yds NNW of X roads in BEAULENCOURT & Cotton's support line. Point 209 yds E and S of the village. Battn. remained in positions gained the previous day. Division on right relieved.	
"	2nd		Battn. in same position. Div on right relieved during the night.	
"	3rd		Battn. in same position. Div on right relieved by Division on right relieved. All quiet on S	
"	4th		B.H.Q. moved to Stayed 500 yds E of VILLARS. Bn at rest. Coy on all left. On S	
VILLARS-AU-FLOS	5th		Side of VILLARS — BEAULENCOURT ROAD. Battn. in rest. Div relieved 35th Div.	
SAILLY-SAILLISEL	6th		Battn. marched by road route to SAILLY-SAILLISEL on LE TRANSLOY. Brigade in Reserve.	
"	7th		Battn. bivouaced at N.W. end of village	
W of MAYENCOURT	7th		Battn. still in reserve. moved by road route to bivouac 1500 yds N.W. of MAYENCOURT	
MANANCOURT EQUANCOURT	8th	4 a.m.	Battn. marched to EQUANCOURT via MANINCOURT and ETRICOURT.	
HEUDECOURT		9 p.m.	Marched to HEUDECOURT via FINS. Brigade relieved 62nd Brigade. 6" Here. Bn. relieved 1st Lincolns in support. Bn. H.Q. 500 yds N.W. of HEUDECOURT. C. & D Coy front. A & D in reserve. C. Coy sunken Rd. 500 yds W of REVELON. B Coy in BROWN LINE A & D in support 10 C & D Bde. 200 yds N of HEUDECOURT. Bde in support to 64th Bde.	
HEUDECOURT	9th		Battn. in close support to 64th Bde. Disposition unchanged	
"	10th		" " " " " " "	

WAR DIARY
or
INTELLIGENCE SUMMARY.
(Erase heading not required.)

Army Form C. 2118.

Instructions regarding War Diaries and Intelligence Summaries are contained in F. S. Regs., Part II. and the Staff Manual respectively. Title pages will be prepared in manuscript.

Place	Date	Hour	Summary of Events and Information	Remarks and references to Appendices
NEUDECOURT	14	—	Batt. in support 1" KRRC Batt. furnishing Bth relief bn' Bn. Bn.H.Q. D & B.coy dispositions unchanged. A" coy details to Barrow line R of NEUDECOURT. C coy in support. Coyd.found (coy stays) front at PEIZIEN	
"	15	9pm	Relieved 1" KRRC in the Lyr sub. sects. of NEUDECOURT A B & D coys in front line. B.H.Q. in BRAGGARD in Fuding cutting. 300 yds S.E. of RAILTON x ROADS	
"	16	10—	Enemy attack - repulsed on A Coy's Gleen Lay C Coy in support attacking on the Butte Enemy front. enemy attacked in waves 8 am 10. lyr and Hannevequin en'ms also off.	
"	16		Dispositions unchanged for no aller eff.	
"	17		In lyr front sub. sect. Dispositions unchanged. Relieved by 1" QUEENS R. 33" Div at night. Batt. moved back to camp S. of NEUDECOURT.	
HARNECOURT	17		In camp E of HARNECOURT. Camp relief on R afternoon.	
"	17	8.30p	Fired off to assembly parties in fields R the camp due to enemy bombing grand manners.	
NEUDECOURT	18	6.20am	B.H.Q. in cutting 300yds E of RAILTON	
"	18		Two Batts. participated in competition and troops take place at 3 Cy. gave & to move on SPENY. O & C Coys in FRONT trenches B.H.Q. AUDENY CUTTING 600 yrs N of PARLICE	
PELUCE	19		Batt. relieved ٧ at night by 1st QUEENS 33" Div. Batt. moved C.E. to ETRICOURT	

WAR DIARY or INTELLIGENCE SUMMARY

Army Form C. 2118.

Place	Date	Hour	Summary of Events and Information	Remarks and references to Appendices
ETRICOURT	20.		Battn. at rest in BILLETS. No training.	
"	21.		"	
"	22.		"	
"	23.		"	
"	24.	10 a.m.	Bn. Bn. Tr. addressed by G.O.C. Division	
"	"	4.30 p.m.	Battn. moved by march route to SOREL-LE-GRAND to huts/tents	
SOREL LE-GRAND	25th	9 p.m.	Battn. moved up to front line GAUCHE WOOD sector. Battn. relieved 10th Sherwoods + 2 Coys of 1st Border Regt. A,B,C Coys in front line, front of GAUCHE WOOD. D Coy in support in Sunken Rd. 800 yds S of GOUZEAUCOURT. Bn. H.Q. in Sunken Rd.	
GAUCHE WOOD	26		Battn. in GAUCHE WOOD sector. dispositions unchanged	
"	27		"	
"	28		"	
"	29	3.30 a.m.	Attack, in conjunction with troops on either flank. Objective GONNELIEU - VILLERS GUISLAIN Rd. B,C,D Coys in front line in support. D Coy reached CROSS POST 200 yds short of objective, B Coy held up by M.G. fire. Enemy retired at dawn. Battn. pushed up to the objective + pushed patrols out 15 Other ranks A, B, D Coy in GRASS STREET B. H.Q. CROSS POST, C Coy in spt. near CROSS POST.	
VILLERS GUISLAN	30.			

Army Form C. 2118.

WAR DIARY
or
INTELLIGENCE SUMMARY

(Erase heading not required.)

Instructions regarding War Diaries and Intelligence Summaries are contained in F. S. Regs., Part II. and the Staff Manual respectively. Title Pages will be prepared in manuscript.

Place	Date	Hour	Summary of Events and Information	Remarks and references to Appendices
	10-9-18		Casualties during the Month of Sept 1918. OFFICERS. Lt. A.J.H.Ford. Killed 18-9-18 2nd Lt. J.H. Howard. Wounded. 18-9-18. " W. Boykins " " " D.M. Christie " " " W.W. Weall " 29-9-18. OTHER RANKS. Killed. 21 Wounded 191 Missing 4 216. [signature] Lt. Col Comdg. 6th/th Leicestershire Regt.	

2449 Wt. W14957/M90 750,000 1/16 J.B.C. & A. Forms/C.2118/12.

CONFIDENTIAL.

WAR DIARY.

6th (Ser.) Batt. Leicestershire Regiment.

FROM Oct. 1st TO Oct. 31st 1918.

Army Form C. 2118.

WAR DIARY
or
INTELLIGENCE SUMMARY.
(Erase heading not required.)

Place	Date	Hour	Summary of Events and Information	Remarks and references to Appendices
	OCTOBER			
VICKERS GUISLAIN	1		Battalion in Support. Bn.H.Q. at CROSS POST 600 yds W of VICKERS GUISLAIN A,B & D Coys in GROSS STREET. C Coy in Reserve at CROSS POST.	
"	2		Relieved by 7th KRRC at night. Battn. moved back to Reserve in Sunken Road foc 400 yds S. of GOUZEAUCOURT.	
GOUZEAUCOURT	3		Battalion Reorganising. Received draft of 105 O.R.	
"	4		" " "	
"	5		Enemy retired. Battn. moved forward. Crossed CANAL DE L'ECOURT at BANTEAUZELLE	
			Battn. in Bde. Support in HINDENBURG LINE 600 yds E of the canal	
BANTEAUZELLE	6		" " " "	
"	7	2200	" moved off to Assembly Positions 600 yds N of MONT COUVEZ FARM	
MONT COUVEZ	8	0515	" attacked BEAUVOIS LINE. Captured all objectives including 430 prisoners & 4 Field Guns. All Coys in front line. Bn. H.Q. in BEAUVOIS front line.	
MEZIERE FM.	9		Dispositions unchanged. 17th DIV passed through. Bn. H.Q. moved to MEZIERE FM.	
CAULKERY	10		Battn. marched to CAULKERY via WARLINCOURT & SELVIGNY.	

Army Form C. 2118.

WAR DIARY
or
INTELLIGENCE SUMMARY.
(Erase heading not required.)

Place	Date	Hour	Summary of Events and Information	Remarks and references to Appendices
CAULLERY	OCTOBER 11		Battalion in Poor Billets. Reorganising	
"	12		" " " " Training	
"	13		" " " " "	
"	14		" " " " "	
"	15		" " " " "	
"	16		" " " " "	
"	17		" " " " "	
"	18		" " " " "	
"	19		" " " " "	
"	20		" " " " "	
"	21		" " " " "	
"	22	0930	Battn. marched to INCHY 2nd Lieut. CAUDRY, + ARDENCOURT.	
"			Rested at INCHY 3 hours.	
"		1530	Moved forward to Assembly Position 800 yds N of AMERVAL	
AMERVAL	23	0730	Attack. Battn. passed through 7th LEIC. R. + 1st WILTS R. to 2nd Objective	
			Objectives gained including VENDIGIES-AU-BOIS + DUKE'S WOOD.	
			62nd Bde. passed through Battn. + continued the advance.	

Army Form C. 2118.

WAR DIARY
or
INTELLIGENCE SUMMARY.
(Erase heading not required.)

Place	Date	Hour	Summary of Events and Information	Remarks and references to Appendices
	OCTOBER			
VENDIGIES-AU-BOIS	24	0530	Batn. moved forward, in Bde Support, to POIX-du-NOID.	
"	"	1630	moved back into billets at VENDIGIES-AU-BOIS.	
"	25	2000	Batn. relieved 64th INF BDE in front line 2 KM. N.E. of POIX-du-NOID	
POIX du NOID	26		Relieved by 12 MANCHESTER R. 17th DIV. moved back to billets in ORVILLERS.	
ORVILLERS	27		Batn. in Billets. Reorganising.	
"	28		" " " "	
"	29		Relieved 9th (Duke of Wellington) Regt. in Support. B + C Coys in front in Trench. D Coy in Spt in Sunken Road. A Coy in BRICKYARD E. of POIX. Bn. H.Q. in POIX du NOID.	
POIX du NOID	30		Batn. in Support. Dispositions Unchanged	
"	31		" " " "	
			Trench Strength 14 officers 340 O.R.	

CONFIDENTIAL.

WAR DIARY

OF

6th Bn Leicestershire Regiment.

FROM 1st November 1918.   TO   30th November 1918.

WAR DIARY or INTELLIGENCE SUMMARY

Army Form C. 2118.

(Erase heading not required.)

Instructions regarding War Diaries and Intelligence Summaries are contained in F.S. Regs., Part II. and the Staff Manual respectively. Title pages will be prepared in manuscript.

Place	Date	Hour	Summary of Events and Information	Remarks and references to Appendices
POIX du NORD	1st		Battalion in Brigade Support Bn C Coy forward in sunken Road S.E. of POIX du NORD. D Coy support in sunken Road S.E. of POIX du NORD.	
"	2nd		In Bn Support. A Coy returned to Bivouacs S.E. of POIX	
"		1930	Relieved by 12th Manchester Regt. Battalion after relief marched to billets in ORVILLERS	
ORVILLERS	3rd		Battalion resting	
"	4th	1235	Battalion marched off for assembly positions	
"	"	1635	" " rested for him W of ENGLE FONTAINE – marched to FUTOY.	
FUTOY	5th	0500	B.H.Q. in FUTOY. Coys extend from ENGLE FONTAINE – BAVIE ROAD.	
"			Haustedts to assembly position 1030 pm N.E. of FUTOY. Coys to enemy withdrawal attack not carried out, took up place S Bavicourt – musket of road	
			LOCQUIGNOL to LA TETE NOIR	
LA TETE NOIR	6th	0330	Road to assembly position. Crossed R. Rhon SAMBRE at BERLAIMONT by footbridge over damaged LOCK. Unable to advance owing to M.G. fire. Battn in line astern D Coy on the right B Coy on the left	

Army Form C. 2118.

WAR DIARY
or
INTELLIGENCE SUMMARY.
(Erase heading not required.)

Instructions regarding War Diaries and Intelligence Summaries are contained in F. S. Regs., Part II. and the Staff Manual respectively. Title pages will be prepared in manuscript.

Place	Date	Hour	Summary of Events and Information	Remarks and references to Appendices
LA TETE NOIRE	6th	1100	Bn. able to advance A, D Coys moved through AULNOYE to objective main road 1000 yds N E of AULNOYE. B Coy mopped up AYMERIES village & stand of timber but unable to locate enemy with 7th D.L.I. Regt on right but unable to get touch with 5th Div. on left. Casualties during day — 27 O.R.	
AULNOYE	7th	0630	Advance continued under Enemy Barrage. In Bde support. moved through BACHANT to Rail line 200 yds E of the village Bn H.Q. in BACHANT. 64th Bde passed through 151st Bde.	
		1900	Batn. ordered to march into BERLAIMONT.	
BERLAIMONT	8th		Batn. resting & reorganising	
"	9th		" " "	
"	10th		" " "	
"	11th	1245	Moved by route march to BEAUFORT. At dusk Battalion found 3 piquets on road E of BEAUFORT — C Coy as Outpost Company.	

Army Form C. 2118.

WAR DIARY
or
INTELLIGENCE SUMMARY.
(Erase heading not required.)

Instructions regarding War Diaries and Intelligence Summaries are contained in F. S. Regs., Part II. and the Staff Manual respectively. Title pages will be prepared in manuscript.

Place	Date	Hour	Summary of Events and Information	Remarks and references to Appendices
BEAUFORT	12		Company training & Sports	
"	13		Musketry & Economy	
"	14		Company training	
"	15		" "	
"	16		Battalion parades & Brigade Ceremonial Parade	
"	17		" " and Parades in Trenches	
"	18		Brigade Tactical Exercise	
"	19		Coy Training & Sports	
"	20		" " "	
"	21		" " "	
"	22		" " "	
"	23		Brigade Ceremonial Parade	
"	24		Divl Series & Sports	
"	25		Company Training & "	
"	26		Training General	

Army Form C. 2118.

WAR DIARY
or
INTELLIGENCE SUMMARY.
(Erase heading not required.)

Place	Date	Hour	Summary of Events and Information	Remarks and references to Appendices
BEAUFORT	24		Company Training & Sports	
	29		" " " "	
	29		Brigade Ceremonial Parade Divine Service & Sports	
	30		Church Parade	
			H. Martin Killed	
			26 " Wounded	
			2-12-16.	

Colonel H. Col.
Commdg 6th Yorks Regt.

CONFIDENTIAL.

WAR DIARY

OF

6th Bn Leicestershire Regiment.

FROM:- 1st December 1918.   TO:- 31st December 1918.

Army Form C. 2118.

WAR DIARY
or
INTELLIGENCE SUMMARY.
(Erase heading not required.)

Place	Date	Hour	Summary of Events and Information	Remarks and references to Appendices
BEAUFORT.	1-12-18		Brigade Route march + Recreation.	
"	2-12-18		Brigade marched to PONT SUR SAMBRE to bil KING. Coy training + games.	
"	3		"	
"	4		"	
"	5		Brigade ceremonial day + games.	
"	6		Divine Service + Recreation.	
"	7		Brigade Route march + Same.	
"	8		Coy training + games.	
"	9		Batts + Interior economy.	
"	10		Battalion Cross Country Run + Sports.	
"	11		Coy training + Recreation.	
"	12		Division commenced move to CAVILLON AREA.	
"	13		Batt proceeded by march route to BERLAIMONT.	
BERLAIMONT.	14		" " " " VENDEGIES	
VENDEGIES	15		" " " " INCHY.	
INCHY.	16		Batt entrained, proceeded to FERRIERS, detrained + proceeded by march route to GUIGNEMICOURT, village allotted to Batt in CAVILLON AREA.	
GUIGNEMICOURT	17		Improvement of existing billets + games.	
"	18		"	
"	19		"	

Army Form C. 2118.

WAR DIARY or INTELLIGENCE SUMMARY.

(Erase heading not required.)

Place	Date	Hour	Summary of Events and Information	Remarks and references to Appendices
AVIGNEM ICOURT	20.12.18		Interior Economy & Games.	
"	21		Coy Training & Games	
"	22		Divine Service & Refreshion	
"	23		Baths - Coy Training & Games	
"	24		Preparing Huts in new Camp for men's Xmas Dinner.	
"	25		Xmas Service. Xmas Dinner & Games.	
"	26		Recreational Training. Watching R.E.'s constructing new Camp.	
"	27		Prepared Recreational Training. do	
"	28		Company Pay & Interior Economy. do	
"	29		Divine Service & Recreation do	
"	30		Coy Training & Games do	
"	31		do do	

Steenyk.   0/4o.   0/ac.
              1/36.   1/4o.

J.R. Rundlett
Lieut Col.
Comdg. 6th Bn. Leicestershire Regt.

CONFIDENTIAL.

WAR DIARY

OF

6th. Batt. Leicestershire Regiment.

FROM:- 1st January 1919. TO:- 31st January 1919.

WAR DIARY
or
INTELLIGENCE SUMMARY.

(Erase heading not required.)

Army Form C. 2118.

Place	Date	Hour	Summary of Events and Information	Remarks and references to Appendices
GUIGNEMICOURT	1/1/19		Coy Training & Recreation	
"	2/1/19		do	
"	3/1/19		C.O. Cs address to Brigade at BOVELLES	
"	4/1/19		Divnl School Recreation	
"	5/1/19		Recreational Training & Education	
"	6/1/19		Coy Training & Recreation	
"	7/1/19		Recreational Training & Education	
"	8/1/19		Coy Training & Games	
"	9/1/19		Coy Training & Recreation	
"	10/1/19		Both Team vs Roy Cnrs Score/A Game in second Run	
"	11/1/19		Divl Inspection Ceremony Rugby Games	
"	12/1/19		Divn to Divnl Recreation	
"	13/1/19		Coy Training & Recreation	
"			Divn by 1st Echelon Educators of Cables	
"			Conversion of Nth Cables at BOVELLES	
"	14/1/19		Remainder of Bttn Coy Training Games	
"	15/1/19		Recreational Training & Education	
"	16/1/19		Coy Training & Recreation	
"	17/1/19		Recreational Training & Education	
"	18/1/19		Brigadiers address to Brigade at ROVELLES	
"	19/1/19		Divnl School Recreation	
"	20/1/19		Recreational Training & Education	
"			Coy Training & Games	

Army Form C. 2118.

WAR DIARY
or
INTELLIGENCE SUMMARY.
(Erase heading not required.)

Instructions regarding War Diaries and Intelligence Summaries are contained in F. S. Regs., Part II. and the Staff Manual respectively. Title pages will be prepared in manuscript.

Place	Date	Hour	Summary of Events and Information	Remarks and references to Appendices
GUIGNEMICOURT	21/1/19		Recreational Training & Education	
"	22		Coy Training & Games	
"	23		Recreational Training & Education	
"	24		Pay. Interior Economy. Baths & Games	
"	25		Divine Service & Recreation	
"	26		Recreational Training & Education	
"	27		Coy Training & Games	
"	28		Recreational Training & Education	
"	29		Coy Training & Games	
"	30		Recreational Training & Education	
"	31		Pay. Interior Economy. Games	

Strength
Offrs. 31.
O.Rs. 792.

J.C. Burnett
Lt Col
OC 1/6 Northumberland Regt

CONFIDENTIAL

WAR

DIARY

OF

6th Batt. Leicestershire Regiment.

FROM:- 1st February 1919.   TO:- 28th February 1919.

Army Form C. 2118.

WAR DIARY
or
INTELLIGENCE SUMMARY.
(Erase heading not required.)

6th Bn Leicestershire Regt

Place	Date	Hour	Summary of Events and Information	Remarks and references to Appendices
GUIGNEMICOURT	1-2-19		Coy Inspection & Interior Economy.	
"	2-		Divine service & Recreation.	
"	3-		Education Classes & Recreational Training.	
"	4-		Coy Training & Sports.	
"	5-		Education Classes, Recreational Training.	
"	6-		Batt Coys Country Run & Games.	
"	7-		Education Classes, Recreational Training.	
"	8-		Coy Inspection, Paft & Interior Economy.	
"	9-		Divine Service & Recreation.	
"	10-		Coy Training & Games.	
"	11-		Education Classes & Recreational Training.	
"	12-		Battalion Route March & Recreation.	
"	13-		Education Classes, Recreational Training.	
"	-		Batt Obst Course, Team Games 1st & 2nd Individual Prizes in Brigade C.C. Run.	
"	14-		Coy Training & Games.	
"	15-		Coy Inspection Paft & Interior Economy.	
"	16-		Divine Service & Recreation.	
"	17-		Education Classes & Recreational Training.	
"	18-		Coy Training & Games.	
"	19-		Education Classes, Recreational Training.	
"	20-		Battalion Route March & Recreation.	
"	21-		Education Classes & Recreational Training.	
"	22-		Coy Inspection Paft & Interior Economy.	
"	23-		Divine Service & Recreation.	
"	24-		Coy Training, Baths & Games.	
"	25-		Education Classes & Recreational Training.	Strength OFFICERS 22. O/Rs 435.
"	26-		do do	
"	27-		Antitank Demn. March & Marathon.	
"	28		Education Classes & Recreational Training.	

Milner Capt
Comdg 6th Leicestershire Regt.

WAR DIARY
or
INTELLIGENCE SUMMARY.

Army Form C. 2118.

Place	Date	Hour	Summary of Events and Information	Remarks and references to Appendices
GUIGNEMICOURT	1-3-19		Coy Inspection. Interior Economy + Pay.	
"	2-		Divin to search + Resertion	
"	3-		Educational. Resertional drawn 9-	
"	4-		Coy training. Same	
"	5-		Educational classes + Resertion	
"	6-		Coy training + Same	
"	7-		Educational classes + Resertion	
"	8-		Battalion moved from GUIGNEMICOURT + closed up with 3rd Div field Regt at FERRIERES	
FERRIERES	9-		Church service + Recreation	
"	10-		Coy training, Reorganisation. Same	
"	11-		Same	
"	12-		Same	
"	13-		Coy training + Same	
"	14-		"	
"	15-		Coy + Bn Inspections, Interior Economy.	
"	16-		Divin'l service + Recreation.	
"	17-		Coy training + Same	
"	18-		"	
"	19-		Battalion Route march Same	
"	20-		Coy training Same	
"	21-		Coy + Bn Interior Economy Same	
"	22-		Divin'l service + Recreation	
"	23-		Coy training + Same	
"	24-		"	
"	25-		Battalion Route march Same	
"	26-		Coy training + Same	
"	27-		Bn Interior Economy Baths	
"	28-		Divin'l service + Recreation	
"	30-			
"	31-			3 Officers + 80 ORs despatched to 266 Regt to Coy DUNKIRK

www.ingramcontent.com/pod-product-compliance
Lightning Source LLC
Chambersburg PA
CBHW081533160426
43191CB00011B/1749